JAMESTOWN

FIRST ENGLISH COLONY

JAMESTOWN

MARSHALL W. FISHWICK

MO NACANS

MANN

POWHATAN
Held this state & fashion when Capt. Smith
was deliuered to him prisoner

MAR=
GOAGS

CHI=
WONS

P

O

W

H

A

T

Powhatan.

James
towne

CHES

Cape Henry

Cape Charles

Smyths Ila

KVSKA

Scale

THE

VIRGINIAN SEA

JAMESTOWN

BY THE EDITORS OF
AMERICAN HERITAGE
The Magazine of History

AUTHOR
MARSHALL W. FISHWICK

CONSULTANT
PARKE ROUSE, JR.
Executive Director, Jamestown Foundation

PUBLISHED BY
AMERICAN HERITAGE PUBLISHING CO., INC.

BOOK TRADE AND INSTITUTIONAL DISTRIBUTION BY
HARPER & ROW

FIRST ENGLISH COLONY

This portrait of Captain John Smith in light armor is based on a contemporary engraving.

FOREWORD

Like anxious latecomers to a feast, the English shouldered their way into the North American continent long after the Spaniards (1539) and the French (1541) had begun to take their places on these shores.

The odds against the success of the first English colonizers were awesome: they had chosen a part of the continent that had no gold and few friendly Indians. Thus, the initial attempts, under Sir Humphrey Gilbert (1583) and Sir Walter Raleigh (1584) were perhaps expectable failures. The next major effort, the construction of a fort on a malarial peninsula in the James River in 1607, seemed finished three years later when the few surviving settlers straggled aboard rescue ships at Jamestown. But almost immediately, the tiny Virginia colony was replanted, and within a decade, it was firmly established. A century after the founding of Jamestown it was clear that England had won the lion's share of the vast new continent.

That story—how bold Englishmen like the red-bearded Captain John Smith (opposite) succeeded in securing a hold on the New World—is told in the pages of this book. It is illustrated by paintings and maps and sketches made by the colonists themselves and by later artists who have taken advantage of recent historical and archaeological research.

Boldness was one weapon that won Virginia for the English, but there were others as well, including good business judgment and a passion for freedom. It is this heritage of daring and vision, as well as the territory of the Old Dominion itself, that the early Virginians bequeathed to all Americans.

The Editors

RIGHT: *A sturdy hinge manufactured in England is but one of many household items unearthed at Jamestown.*

COLONIAL NATIONAL HISTORICAL PARK

TITLE PAGE: *William Couper's statue of John Smith overlooks the James from the original site of Jamestown.*

BRADLEY SMITH: PHOTO RESEARCHERS

FRONT ENDSHEET: *In Smith's map of Virginia, looking west over Chesapeake Bay, Jamestown (left, center) is nearly lost in Powhatan's empire.*

PRINCETON UNIVERSITY LIBRARY

BACK ENDSHEET: *By 1625 the colony was expanding beyond its low-lying peninsula (center) to the higher and healthier ground of the mainland.*

COLONIAL NATIONAL HISTORICAL PARK
COURTESY WILLIAMSBURG
PAINTING BY SIDNEY KING

COVER: *This portion of the view of Jamestown on the back endsheet focuses on the settlement's first fort.*

COLONIAL NATIONAL HISTORICAL PARK
COURTESY WILLIAMSBURG
PAINTING BY SIDNEY KING

CONTENTS

1	SEADOGS AND COLONISTS	10
2	DREAM OF VIRGINIA	26
3	JAMES FORT	48
4	THE GOLDEN LEAF	66
5	MASSACRE	94
6	MUTINY AND REBELLION	112
7	THE VIRGINIANS	134
	Acknowledgments	150
	Further Reading	151
	Index	152

1

SEADOGS AND COLONISTS

Most voyages from England to the New World, including many described or inspired by Richard Hakluyt, began in the harbors of England's south coast, shown in the sixteenth-century map below. At center, two typical English merchant ships sail before the wind into Plymouth Sound.

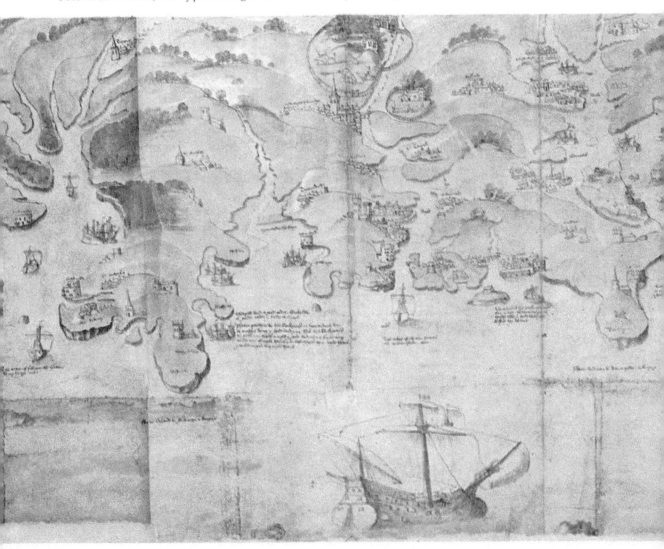

One fine summer day in the year 1580, a young English clergyman swung into the saddle of his horse and set off to meet an old seadog named Thomas Butts. The clergyman, Richard Hakluyt, was twenty-seven years old and had recently received his Master of Arts degree from Oxford University. Now he prepared to leave the comfort of the university to face a ride of two hundred miles over miserable roads.

But he hardly spared a thought for the hazards and hardships of the journey, for the man he was about to meet had been a seaman on one of the first English expeditions to Newfoundland. Young Hakluyt was ready to endure any discomfort in the quest for fresh information on the exploits of English explorers and travelers.

This passion for information had been roused by an older cousin, his

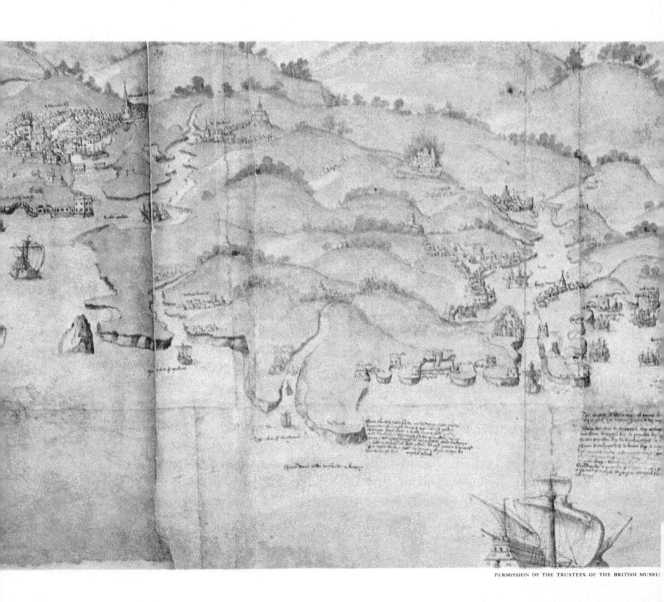

THE PRINCIPALL
NAVIGATIONS, VOIA-
GES AND DISCOVERIES OF THE
English nation, made by Sea or ouer Land,
*to the most remote and farthest distant Quarters of
the earth at any time within the compasse
of these 1500. yeres: Deuided into three
seuerall parts, according to the po-
sitions of the Regions whereunto they were directed.*

The first, conteining the personall trauels of the English vnto *Iudea, Syria, A-
rabia,* the riuer *Euphrates, Babylon, Balsara,* the *Persian* Gulfe, *Ormuz, Chaul,
Goa, Indie,* and many Ilands adioyning to the South parts of *Asia:* together with the like vnto *Egypt,* the chiefest ports and places of *Africa* within and without the Streight of *Gibraltar,* and about the famous Promon-
torie of *Buona Esperança.*

The second, comprehending the worthy discoueries of the English towards
the North and Northeast by Sea, as of *Lapland, Scrikfinia, Corelia,* the Baie
of *S. Nicholas,* the Isles of *Colgoieue, Vaigats,* and *Noua Zembla* toward the
great riuer *Ob,* with the mightie Empire of *Russia,* the *Caspian* Sea, *Georgia,
Armenia, Media, Persia, Boghar* in *Bactria,* & diuers kingdoms of *Tartaria.*

The third and last, including the English valiant attempts in searching almost all the corners of the vaste and new world of *America,* from 73. de-
grees of Northerly latitude Southward, to *Meta Incognita, Newfoundland,*
the maine of *Virginia,* the point of *Florida,* the Baie of *Mexico,* all the Inland of *Noua Hispania,* the coast of *Terra firma, Brasill,* the riuer of *Plate,* to
the Streight of *Magellan:* and through it, and from it in the South Sea to
Chili, Peru, Xalisco, the Gulfe of *California, Noua Albion* vpon the backside
of *Canada,* further then euer any Christian hitherto hath pierced.

*Whereunto is added the last most renowmed English Nauigation,
round about the whole Globe of the earth.*

By *Richard Hakluyt Master of Artes, and Student sometime
of Christ-church in Oxford.*

Imprinted at London by GEORGE BISHOP
and RALPH NEWBERIE, Deputies to
CHRISTOPHER BARKER, Printer to the
Queenes most excellent Maiestie.
1589.

*The title page of Hakluyt's 1589 book of
discovery lists "valiant attempts in searching . . . the vast and new world of America."*

namesake, Richard Hakluyt, who was
a lawyer in London. The older Hakluyt was one of the first Englishmen
to become an expert in geography.
Merchants and trading companies
drew on his fund of knowledge before
setting out on business ventures in
many parts of the world, and they
paid him handsomely for his advice.

England had lagged far behind the
leaders in the great Age of Exploration that spanned the fifteenth and
sixteenth centuries. A small and iso-
lated island, she had taken no part in
the early forays that had enriched the
cities of Italy and had led to the founding of the Portuguese and Spanish empires. The merchandise that England
exported and the goods she imported
were carried in foreign vessels. Her
own small merchant fleet had been
built largely in foreign shipyards. Her
earliest explorers, the Cabots, were
Italians by birth, and even when Englishmen led their own expeditions,
they were usually guided by foreign
navigators.

Young Richard Hakluyt was to
play a large part in changing this. He
became interested in geography while
still a schoolboy. Once, on a visit to
the rooms of his older cousin, who
had become his guardian on the death
of his father in 1557, he recalled: "I
found lying open . . . certain books on
cosmography, with a universal map;
[my cousin] seeing me somewhat curious in the view thereof, began to in-
struct my ignorance . . . he pointed
out all the known seas, gulfs, bays,
straits, capes, rivers . . . and the territories of each part, with declaration
of their special commodities and particular wants."

From school Hakluyt went on to
Oxford University to study for the
ministry, since this would provide him
with an income while he continued his
geographical research. He also set out
to master languages because few texts
on geography had been translated
into, or written in, English.

In addition to reading, however, he followed his cousin's example by collecting more practical information from merchants, from mariners like Thomas Butts, from travelers, and from the reports gathered by trading companies from their agents in foreign countries. He studied the newest maps and globes and corresponded with the leading geographers of his day—men like Mercator and Ortelius, who founded the modern science of geography.

In 1582, Hakluyt published his first collection of material, *Divers Voyages touching the discovery of America*. His aim was to promote the glory of England by awakening his fellow countrymen's interest in exploration and colonization. His approach was completely practical, for he spoke to the solid middle-class merchants, stressing the importance of American colonies to trade. He pointed out that such colonies would provide work for the unemployed, and he listed "Certain Commodities Growing in part of America" that were needed in England. In *Divers Voyages*, he also included maps and the accounts he had so painstakingly gathered from the merchants and mariners of England.

The book created widespread interest, and Hakluyt's hard work was recognized with an official appointment: chaplain to Sir Edward Stafford, the English ambassador at the French court in Paris. Hakluyt used his new appointment to collect accounts of Spanish and French expeditions to the New World, and to gather further information that might be useful to English explorers in America. He talked to everyone who could help him. He sought out exiled Portuguese captains and pilots and became friendly with French and Italian sailors, who showed him animal skins painted by Indians and a piece of a sassafras tree brought from Florida and said to have medicinal qualities.

Soon, Hakluyt's services were needed in England. In 1584, Sir Walter Raleigh recalled him to help persuade

The voyages of John Cabot and his son Sebastian (above) helped establish English claims to America's northeastern coast.

14

A 1542 map made for Henry VIII traces fairly accurately the outlin[e] *of Europe and Africa, but North America (left above) is little mo[re]*

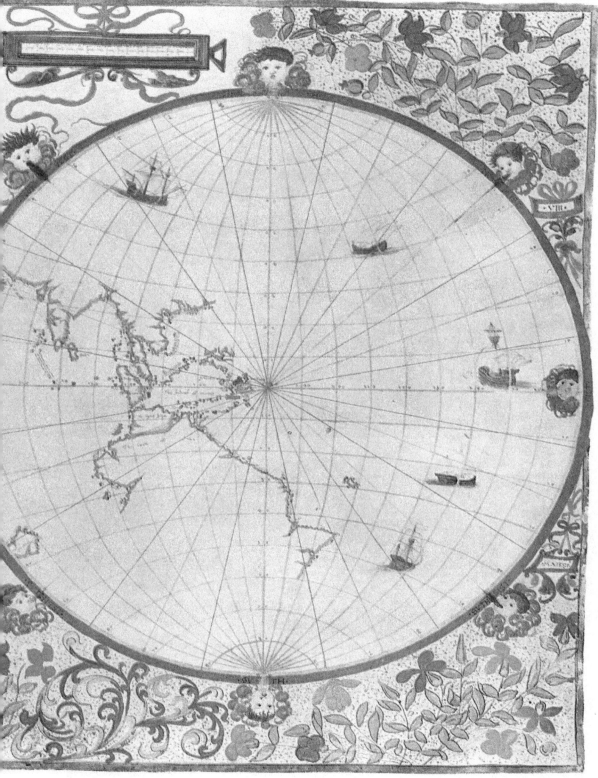

...an a reef blocking the passage to the mysterious and unknown lands of
...e Orient (above), the true objective of most early New World voyages.

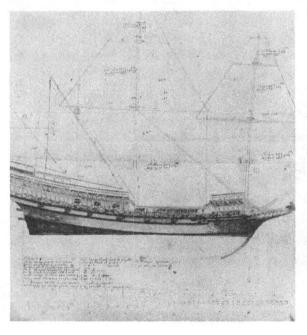

England's sixteenth-century sea power was based on the speed and maneuverability of her well-constructed ships. Three drawings from a 1586 book illustrate shipwrights in ruffs and pantaloons working at their designing boards (top), the hull of a ship compared to a fish (above), and a sail plan (right) for a galleon with a high stern and beaked prow.

16

Queen Elizabeth I to put her money and her influence behind the effort to plant a colony in America. Hakluyt wrote a persuasive secret report (known briefly as *The Discourse on the Western Planting*) which he presented to the queen.

He argued that without colonies England could not hope to match the power of Spain and Portugal. Bases were needed from which English privateers and warships could strike Spanish and Portuguese treasure ships and fishing fleets. And in challenging the might of the great Catholic empires, England would bring glory not only to herself as a nation but to the Protestant cause that she led. But—as always with Hakluyt—there were more practical reasons to be considered. England had to have new markets for her goods and new sources of raw material. Only if prosperous farms and colonies were to be set up on the other side of the Atlantic could such aims be accomplished.

Hakluyt supported all these arguments with figures and details. He listed the types of emigrants most needed in America: carpenters, craftsmen, builders; gardeners to establish vineyards and orchards; soldiers for defense. "Valiant youths rusting and hurtful by lack of employment" could be sent overseas. Anglican clergymen could preach the gospel to the heathen, bringing salvation to untold thousands who had not heard of Christ. His report was never made public; and, in any case, it was aimed at prov-

ing to the hard-headed and close-fisted Elizabeth that Raleigh's colonies could show a profit and increase England's power and prestige.

Hakluyt later popularized the cause he shared with Raleigh in his masterpiece, a huge collection of traveler's accounts called *The Principal Navigations, Voyages, and Discoveries of the English nation . . .* This work, more than any other, helped to direct the nation's increasing interest in exploration and foreign trade, an interest that had been stirring under the Tudor monarchs who ruled sixteenth-century England.

King Henry VIII had pushed the development of a formidable navy; and during the reign of his canny daughter Elizabeth, who succeeded to the throne in 1558, the English became one of the leading sea powers in Europe. English merchant princes and explorers began to dream of riches to be won in distant lands. Trading companies were formed to carry English goods to Russia, the north German towns, Turkey, and the Far East.

Typical of the new breed of Elizabethan adventurer was Francis Drake, the son of a Devon parson. Drake saw himself as the champion of the English people and the Protestant faith against the might of Catholic Spain. With the secret support of Elizabeth, he waged a one-man war against King Philip of Spain, and his name soon became a terrible legend among the Spanish coastal towns. He headed privateering expeditions to the

THE GLORIOUS HOUSE OF TUDOR

During the 118-year-long reign of the Tudor family (1485–1603), England became a leading world power. The second Tudor monarch, Henry VIII (in a confident pose opposite), ruled for thirty-eight years (1509–47) and is today perhaps best remembered for his six wives—two he divorced, two were beheaded, one died of natural causes, one outlived him—and for removing the English Church from control of the Roman pope. After the brief reigns of Edward VI and Mary, Henry's second daughter, Elizabeth I (above, holding the scepter and the cross-topped orb of her office), became queen. In the forty-five years she ruled (1558–1603), English seafarers raided Spain's New World colonies and defeated the Spanish Armada; Shakespeare wrote many of his great plays; and Walter Raleigh founded his Roanoke colony.

18

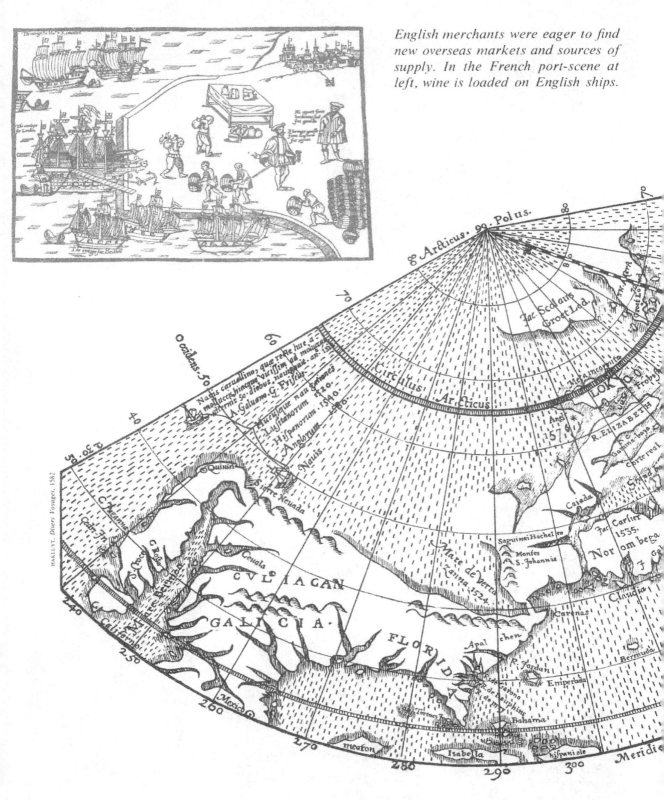

English merchants were eager to find new overseas markets and sources of supply. In the French port-scene at left, wine is loaded on English ships.

A sketchy map, published in 1582 by Hakluyt, shows North America above Florida as a series of islands with inviting water routes to the Orient.

Spanish West Indies, and in 1573, leading his men across the Isthmus of Panama he became the first Englishman to see the Pacific Ocean. Kneeling on the heights of Darien he asked God to give him "life and leave to sail once in an English ship upon that sea." His prayer was answered a few years later when driving south and west before wild Atlantic storms he rounded Cape Horn and took his battered little ship, the *Golden Hind*, up the coast of Chile, plundering the Spanish colonies as he went. By the time he had reached the west coast of Mexico, the *Golden Hind* was laden with treasure.

Fearing that the Spaniards would intercept him if he returned by the same route, Drake sailed west across the Pacific, after landing briefly on the California coast. He reached England on September 26, 1580, the first Englishman to sail around the world. The dramatic feats of Drake and others like him created the mood for Hakluyt's successful efforts to rouse English enthusiasm for overseas adventure.

Yet, though Hakluyt burned to cross the Atlantic, he was fated never to make the journey. While he was publicizing the "western plantation" of colonies, others were taking practical steps toward founding the English empire overseas. The first attempt to colonize the New World was led by Sir Humphrey Gilbert, the son of a Devon gentleman and the half brother of Sir Walter Raleigh. Gilbert was

21

well known for his reckless courage and boundless energy, and he had served a hard apprenticeship against the rebels in Ireland and the Spaniards in the Low Countries. In 1566, he had petitioned Queen Elizabeth, urging that efforts be made to discover "a passage by the north to go to Cataia [Cathay]." This "passage by the north" was the mythical northwest passage that dominated the minds of the English explorers of the New World. But Gilbert's appeal went unanswered, and in 1573, he withdrew from his more active life to prepare for publication his *Discourse of a Discovery for a New Passage to Cataia*.

He claimed that America was the fabulous lost island of Atlantis. And he argued that since there was a passage to the south (the Strait of Magellan) there must logically be a passage to the north, "which," he wrote, "I now take in hand to discover."

Gilbert was not interested only in tapping the riches of Cathay and India through his northwest passage. He also dreamed of founding a colony in the New World, a "western plantation" in America. Others shared the dream; many more were drawn by the golden lure of the Indies. And for both reasons the *Discourse* was widely read and discussed. Finally, in June of 1578, Gilbert received his long-sought charter for the "inhabiting and planting of our people in America." He was instructed to "discover, find, search out, and view such remote, heathen, and barbarous countries and

In 1585, Francis Drake anchored his English fleet in the harbor of Santo Domingo, a Spanish port in the Caribbean, marched his men from the landing at left, and defeated the Spaniards at the city walls. The alligator and tortoise pictured in the bay were killed and eaten by the English raiders.

23

territories not actually possessed by any Christian prince or people." Selling everything he possessed to back the venture, he assembled a small fleet and set sail in November, 1578, only to hurry back to port after a disastrous encounter with Spanish ships in the South Atlantic.

Gilbert spent the next few years trying to repair his fortunes, and he sought the help of his kinsman Raleigh and other "gentlemen of good estimation." He gathered together a new expedition of 260 men (including "mineral men" to search for gold and silver) and five ships, the largest built and crewed at Raleigh's expense.

After his unfortunate attempt at the southern route, Gilbert decided to try the northern route to America, following the "trade way unto New-foundland." Raleigh was ordered by Queen Elizabeth to stay in England—his life was too valuable to risk on such uncertain ventures. But the queen did send Gilbert a present—a gold brooch in the shape of an anchor set with pearls—and her royal blessing. Gilbert's spirits were high as he put to sea on June 11, 1583: it seemed that the time had at last come to find the passage to the East and found a New World colony.

His feelings were not shared by all of his companions. On the second night, without a word of explanation, the captain of the *Bark-Raleigh* turned his ship for home. Soon after, a second ship, the *Swallow*, manned by a crew of cutthroats who had joined the

expedition only to escape prison, deserted in a thick fog. However, Gilbert sailed on, and seven weeks after leaving England, the *Delight*, the *Squirrel*, and the *Golden Hind* sighted the coast of Newfoundland. There the *Swallow*, its crew dressed in new clothes from a plundered fishing vessel, rejoined them —much to Gilbert's astonishment.

Gilbert had little control over his followers. After landing and claiming the territory for England, some of his men deserted. Quarrels broke out among those who remained.

At last, ordering the *Swallow* back to England with a cargo of sick men, Gilbert pushed on toward the mainland of North America. On the seventh day, his ships ran into foul weather and barely escaped wrecking. Two

FOLGER SHAKESPEARE LIBRARY

A 1622 English illustration depicts the hazards of early navigation, with the hand of fate set to jerk a vessel to its briny grave.

days later the *Delight* was driven onto the coast and was lost with most of her men and all her cargo.

The *Golden Hind* and the *Squirrel* tried to sail on, but contrary winds kept them from reaching the coast, and the thick fog and biting cold continued. Provisions were almost exhausted; the men begged to turn back. Finally Gilbert agreed, vowing that he would return the next spring if God now sent them safely home. He ordered his ships to trim their sails for England.

But the adventurers troubles were far from ended. Several days out they were overtaken by a storm that sent huge waves crashing over the decks of the tiny ships, whose sides creaked and groaned under the hammering of tons of water. The men huddled below must have felt that their end was near.

Earlier, Gilbert had moved from the *Golden Hind* to the smaller *Squirrel* in order to explore the coast. Now he refused to leave her, even though she was unseaworthy, saying "I will not forsake my little company going homeward with whom I have passed so many storms and perils." But the *Squirrel* was so overloaded with rigging, guns, and supplies that she was too difficult to handle in the stormy Atlantic. On September 9, the inevitable tragedy overtook her. While the gale continued to batter the ships, the men on the *Golden Hind* could see Gilbert on his little vessel, calmly reading from the book in his hand. "We are as near to heaven by sea as by land," he

Returning from an attempt to settle in North America, Humphrey Gilbert was lost at sea.

shouted cheerfully to them. Later that night a monstrous wave swamped the *Squirrel*, and she sank like a stone.

All night long the *Golden Hind* searched for the lost comrades. But not a fragment nor a single survivor was sighted. The one remaining ship limped into port on September 22.

Gilbert was gone. But his heroism was not in vain. Sir Walter Raleigh decided to carry on with his work. If a northern colony was not practicable, a settlement might be possible in the milder southern climate, and he would be willing to risk his fortune on that.

Nineteen months after the *Golden Hind* had staggered home with the sad tale of Gilbert's death, Raleigh's first company was moving out to sea from Plymouth—bound for the new land across the Atlantic. Richard Hakluyt's dream was at last to become a reality.

2

DREAM OF VIRGINIA

More than any other man, Sir Walter Raleigh was responsible for England's first, insecure toehold on the shores of the New World.

He was born in Devon, the home of many other great Elizabethan adventurers, about 1522. His father was a country gentleman, and like most men of his class, he sent his son to Oxford University. But young Walter was not cut out to be a scholar; at the age of fifteen or sixteen he found a trade more to his liking. He accompanied his mother's cousin, Henry Champernown, to fight with the French Protestants against their Catholic king.

Raleigh served the Protestant cause in France until 1574, when he returned to London to study law (though probably not too seriously). Soon his adventurous spirit grew restless among the dusty textbooks. Four years later, he was off with his half brother, Sir Humphrey Gilbert, on his 1578 expedition. The voyage began and ended

The gem-encrusted armor that Sir Walter Raleigh wore for the 1588 portrait opposite was designed for court functions, not combat.

in trouble. The two sea rovers sailed against the queen's orders—and were fined for their insolence when they returned—and before they had passed the Azores, they were badly mauled by a Spanish squadron. One ship was sunk, and Raleigh was lucky to bring his own battered vessel home intact.

One setback could not dampen his enthusiasm. His fiery energy soon found another outlet in Ireland. Again he followed in the footsteps of Gilbert, who, ten years before as governor of the province of Munster, had suppressed a rebellion with efficiency and ferocity. Raleigh, commanding a company of infantry against the rebels, was even more effective, and in cruelty he was a match for Gilbert. He even advanced a plan for ending the revolt by assassinating all the Irish leaders; fortunately for his own reputation, he was never given the opportunity to put his plan into action.

By the end of 1581 he was back in London with dispatches from Ireland and determined to advance his fortunes at court. Although he had made enemies with his blunt and quarrelsome manner (the year before he went

to Ireland he had been jailed twice for dueling), he also had staunch friends in high places. His work in Ireland had brought him to the attention of important men close to the queen, and his quick wit and his flair for grand gestures soon caught Elizabeth's fancy. The story of Raleigh spreading his expensive cloak over a "plashy place" so that she could cross it dry-shod may not be true, but it is typical of his temper.

Raleigh quickly rose to favor at court. Before long, he was master of huge estates in Ireland and England and held a valuable royal monopoly for licensing the sale of wine throughout the kingdom. But he was not content merely to live the idle life of a courtier. His biographer John Aubrey wrote: "He was no slug; without doubt he had a wonderful waking spirit." It was reputed that he slept only five hours a day; the rest of the time was spent in reading, in conversation, and in business affairs. And after the death of Gilbert on the tragic expedition of 1583, much of Raleigh's business was bound up with fulfilling Gilbert's dream of a New World colony.

In March, 1584, he took over Gilbert's charter for discovering and colonizing "new lands and countries," and within a month he had two ships ready for the first attempt. Forced to remain in England, he chose as commanders Arthur Barlow, who had served with him in Ireland, and Philip Amadas, a relative of England's greatest seaman, John Hawkins. The ships, piloted by the famous Portuguese navigator Simon Fernandez, sailed the privateer's route by the West Indies and Florida and in July dropped anchor off the North Carolina coast.

Barlow later wrote an enthusiastic report of the scene that greeted their land-hungry eyes: "Goodly Woods full of Deer, Conies [rabbits], Hares, and Fowl even in the middest of Summer . . . the highest and reddest Cedars of the world . . . Pines, Cypress, Sassafras, the Lentisk . . . that beareth the rind of black cinnamon."

The explorers landed on Wokoken Island (now called Ocracoke Island), claiming it for Raleigh in the name

An artist of the sixteenth century drew the scene on the opposite page of an expedition's ships in Dover harbor. A more recent artist reconstructed the incident above: from their ship's small boat, men of Raleigh's 1584 expedition hail Indians on the Carolina coast.

of the queen. Three days later they met their first Indians, from whom they received a canoeload of fish in exchange for clothes and trinkets.

The next day more Indians arrived, eager to trade skins and furs for pots and pans and tools of iron, which they had never seen before. Among the Indians was Granganimeo, brother of the local chieftain, Wingina, who had been wounded in a battle and could not make the trip himself. Although the Indians and the Englishmen shared no common language, the explorers questioned Granganimeo and learned —or so they thought—that the territory was called Wingandacoa. (Actually, the chief's brother had not understood what they were saying, and he was commenting, "You wear fine clothes"; but the name stuck.)

Granganimeo also told them that they were not the first Europeans to land on the coast. A white man's ship had been wrecked there years before, and the survivors had lived with the Indians for some time before attempting to sail home in their lifeboats.

The dangers of North Carolina's outer banks are symbolized by wrecks in this illustration of the 1585 voyage. In the bay, an English boat nears Roanoke. The Indian opposite wears a fringed deerskin.

English raiders often attacked Spanish ships bearing New World treasure. Here, the Englishmen (at left) prepare to ram and board.

This explained why many of the Indians were red-haired.

Later, Barlow visited the island of Roanoke ("shell money"), where he found Granganimeo's wife living in a village of cedar-built houses. After being royally entertained, he and his men returned to the ships and set sail for England, taking with them two of the Indians, Manteo and Wanchese.

While his two captains were away,

Raleigh was making every effort to interest Elizabeth in his venture. He summoned Hakluyt from Paris to write his confidential report, and he discussed the project with everyone who might be able to influence the queen.

What Elizabeth thought of Hakluyt's discourse is not known. However, when Amadas and Barlow reached England with their glowing

32

description of Wingandacoa and its "mild, gentle, loving, and faithful" natives, the Virgin Queen allowed Raleigh to rename the new American territory Virginia in her honor. In exchange she honored Raleigh with a knighthood.

Raleigh plunged with renewed vigor into preparations for a second and larger expedition. Seven ships were fitted out, and Raleigh's cousin, the famous sea rover Sir Richard Grenville, was selected to lead them. Several other distinguished men were among the "one hundred householders" who assembled for the trip: Thomas Cavendish, who was later to repeat Drake's voyage around the globe; John White, a talented artist and map maker; Thomas Hariot, whom Raleigh had brought from Oxford University to teach him science and who was to become the most famous scientist of the day; and Ralph Lane, a veteran of the Irish trouble, who was to be governor of the new colony. Amadas and Fernandez had also decided to return to Virginia, and the two Indians, Manteo, now a firm friend of the white men, and Wanchese, their bitter enemy, were being taken home.

On April 9, 1585, Grenville's little fleet weighed anchor and made sail for Virginia. But Grenville was less interested than Raleigh in long-range plans. He was determined to make a quick profit from the trip. Before he reached the West Indies, he had captured two Spanish vessels and had

ransomed the wealthier passengers. When he touched at Hispaniola for supplies, he sold part of the cargoes, keeping the remainder for the new colony. Finally, well satisfied, he headed his ships for the mainland.

They reached Wokoken Island on June 26, but before landing the colonists, Grenville decided to explore the mainland. However, in crossing the great sand bar that runs along the coast, he grounded his flagship, *Tyger*, and almost wrecked her. The crew managed to refloat her and sail on,

Sir Richard Grenville turned his 1585 voyage to and from Raleigh's Virginia colony into profitable raids on Spain's high-seas trade.

but sea water, gushing through her sprung planks, ruined the wheat and the other supplies in her hold—a loss that was not felt until later.

On the mainland, Grenville discovered three Indian villages, where he and his men were met with hospitality and friendship. But at one of the villages, Aquascogoc, a silver cup was stolen by one of the Indians, and Grenville ordered Amadas to burn the houses and crops in retaliation. Far from cowing the Indians, Amadas' action turned them against the white men, with disastrous results for the colonists.

The leaders of the expedition decided to establish their settlement on Roanoke Island, near Granganimeo's village. After Lane and his men had disembarked on the island and had begun to build a fort and living quarters, Grenville prepared to return to England. He left on August 25, promising to come back the following spring with supplies. On his return voyage he overtook a Spanish treasure ship and boarded her. He sailed her back to England in triumph, and Raleigh sold her cargo to cover the cost of his expedition.

Meanwhile, on Roanoke, Ralph

Roanoke's colonists went hungry, although the nearby waters teemed with fish. In the water color opposite, John White, the second Roanoke governor, showed Indians fishing with spears and nets. His paintings are the first true views of North American life.

Lane was proving to be an ideal governor of the colony. He was an experienced leader of men and a stern disciplinarian. But his efforts to found a permanent "plantation" were hampered from the beginning. Although many of the new colonists had seen military service, none of them had any experience as farmers. So while they could defend themselves against attack by the Indians or by the Spaniards, whose colonies were a few days' sail away on the Florida coast, they were soon running short of food. Most of the supplies they had brought with them had been spoiled in the near wreck of the *Tyger*, and after the burning of Aquascogoc, they could no longer depend on the Indians for food. And it was too late in the year to plant crops of their own.

Despite the difficulties they faced, the new settlers were soon hard at work. Hariot and White began to map the territory around the base on Roanoke. The scientist also collected material for a report on the animals, plants, and minerals of the area, while White sketched everything he encountered, including many scenes of Indian life. Lane sent off an exploring party to investigate Indian reports of a better harborage to the north (Chesapeake Bay), and early in the following year he prepared to lead a gold-hunting party up the Roanoke River.

The colonists' continual and sometimes violent demands for food had by this time turned Chief Wingina against them. Granganimeo, their closest link with the Indians, had died, and Wingina began stirring up trouble among neighboring tribes. So when Lane and his gold hunters left the settlement, Wingina persuaded his Indian allies to set up a blockade of the sixty white men left on Roanoke Island. Then he ordered the tribes living along Lane's route to hide in the woods, taking all their food supplies with them. Lane's little expedition, growing hungrier with each day's march, passed through one deserted village after another. At last, in order to stay alive, they had to kill and eat two mastiffs they had brought with them. Even so, they marched on until a skirmish with an Indian war party persuaded Lane that their position was hopeless. Starving and empty-handed, they began the dreary trek back to the settlement.

Wingina had boasted that Lane would perish in the woods, so the successful return of the gold hunters, desperate and barely alive though they were, was a blow to the chief.

By this time, there was perilously little food left on the island. The only hope for the settlers was to split up into small groups and fend for themselves until Grenville arrived with relief. One party went south to Croatoan Island to watch for ships; the rest were scattered about to search for plants on the mainland and shellfish along the shores.

Wingina was delighted with the success of his blockade. He had too much respect for the English guns to

In John White's painting of a spirited Indian festival held near Roanoke, natives dance about posts carved at the top to represent human heads.

risk an attack, but now, with his enemy scattered, he prepared to go on the warpath. But his plan was betrayed to Lane by the son of a friendly chief, whom the Englishmen were holding as a hostage. Lane decided to attack first. With a party of his toughest men, he raided Wingina's village, killed the chief and several of his lieutenants, and broke up his army.

For the time, the threat of an Indian massacre was over, but the problem of food still remained unsolved. However, help was at hand. A few days after the raid, the lookout party on Croatoan caught sight of sails over the horizon. Before long a flotilla of twenty-three ships, led by Sir Francis

The sixteenth-century English farming family pictured above at mealtime looks happy and contented. But land was hard for them to obtain; the New World sounded wonderfully rich despite its hazards.

Drake, was swinging at anchor off Roanoke Island.

Quite by chance, Drake had decided to visit the settlement after making a successful plundering raid on the Spanish colonies to the south. When he was told of the desperate plight of Lane's party, he offered to take them back to England. After much discussion, Lane agreed, although he was reluctant to abandon the island, and he still wanted to explore Chesapeake Bay. So, six weeks later, Raleigh's first colonists landed in Portsmouth with little to show for their efforts but Hariot's report, White's drawings, and a strange new vegetable called the potato.

Meanwhile, Grenville, who had set out some weeks before with the promised supplies, arrived at Roanoke Island to find the colony deserted. He knew nothing of the trouble with the Indians or of Lane's decision to leave. Search parties were dispatched to look for the missing colonists, but they reported no trace of them. So Grenville sailed for England, leaving fifteen men with two years' supplies to hold the island for the Crown.

The story of Lane's troubles and his failure to find gold discouraged many who had been interested in Raleigh's venture. Even Raleigh himself had grown a little more cautious. However, he was still determined to found a colony in Virginia, and in 1586, he formed a company to settle a new site. Chesapeake Bay was selected—probably on Lane's advice—because the shoal waters around Roanoke were dangerous for ships, and the hostility of the Indians would make life difficult. Still, three members of Lane's expedition were ready to return, and a group of nineteen men, including Richard Hakluyt, agreed to finance the attempt.

The artist John White, now a veteran colonizer, was selected as governor of the new colony, with twelve assistants to act as his council. Three of these councilors would remain in England to make sure that supplies were sent regularly to the colonists.

Something had been learned from the earlier failures. It was obvious that a purely military expedition like Lane's could not hope to survive; the settlers had to be able to support themselves in the wilderness. Plans were made to include whole families in the new group, and to attract recruits, a bounty of five hundred acres of land was promised to each settler. Many of the 150 settlers who joined White were farmers who had sold everything they owned in England in hope of a new life across the Atlantic.

The expedition sailed in three ships in May, 1587, and reached Roanoke Island in late July. Here they were supposed to pick up Grenville's garrison before pressing on to Chesapeake Bay. However (except for a single skeleton), there was no trace of the fifteen men. White wrote that the fort had burned down and was "overgrown with melons of divers sorts." Grass was sprouting inside the houses.

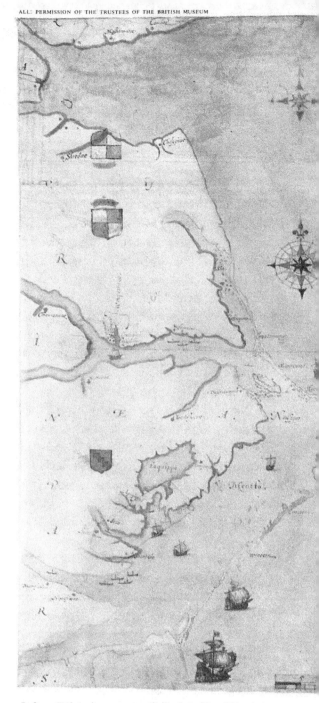

White had been quarreling with the pilot, Fernandez, since the voyage began. He perhaps suspected that Fernandez was working for the Spanish Crown: and certainly Fernandez had been behaving in a suspicious way. He had almost abandoned his ship after an accident in the Bay of Biscay, and he had nearly wrecked her off the North Carolina coast. Now he claimed that it was too late in the year to carry on to Chesapeake Bay.

The settlers had no choice but to make shift as best they could. They repaired the fort and houses and built new ones, but they were hampered by the lack of proper equipment. And worn-out tools could not be replaced unless a relief ship was sent from England. The food supply was scanty, and the water was often foul. Scurvy and dysentery took their toll: nearly a third of the settlers died in the first

John White's map of Raleigh's Virginia, from Chesapeake Bay to what is now Cape Lookout, North Carolina, includes seven English ships and eleven Indian dugouts, with Roanoke (center) and Croatoan islands in red. At top are three White nature studies: a loggerhead turtle, a pelican, and a butterfly.

40

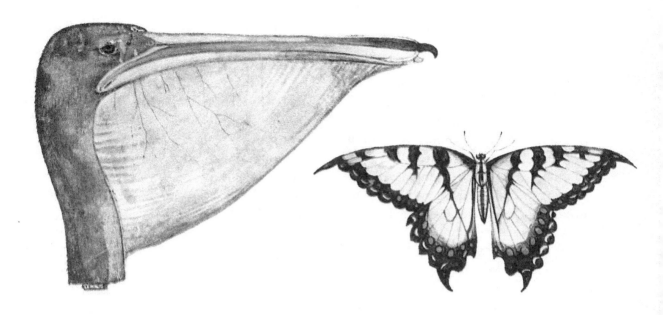

six months. The Indians also remained hostile. Soon after the settlers arrived, one of the councilors, George Howe, was ambushed and killed while catching crabs along the shore.

Yet there were some bright moments amid the gloom. In August, the friendly Indian Manteo was christened and then appointed, as Raleigh's vassal, Lord of Roanoke and the surrounding territory. And five days later, Governor White's daughter, Eleanor Dare, gave birth to a girl who was named Virginia in honor of the colony. She was the first English child to be born in America.

However, it was soon clear that unless someone was sent to England to fetch help, the new colony would perish. Volunteers were called for, but no one could be persuaded to make the perilous Atlantic crossing in the small boat (Fernandez was deter-

mined to go privateering in the West Indies and would not take a messenger to England first). At last the council appointed White as its representative. They hoped that with his daughter and granddaughter in Virginia, he would make every effort to return quickly with the supplies.

White's mission was doomed to failure. When he reached England on November 5, he found the country preparing for a life-and-death struggle with Spain. King Philip II was outfitting his great Armada, and few people had time to think of anything else. Still, Raleigh turned a willing ear to White's demands and began to assemble supplies for the colonists. But before the relief ships, which were to be led once more by Grenville, could get under way, Elizabeth's Privy Council decreed that no merchant ships were to leave port. Crews and cargoes were to be pressed into service against the Armada.

However, Raleigh managed to persuade the government to let White sail, and in April, 1588, he set out with two small ships. But once again he was to be disappointed. His crews decided to go privateering, and White was helpless to stop them. After several unsuccessful clashes with Spanish ships, the renegades turned tail and returned to England.

By this time, Raleigh's services were needed in the defense of his country. He was sent to Ireland to organize land defenses against a possible attack in that direction, and his lieutenant, Grenville, joined the English squadrons collecting in the Channel to meet the Spanish Armada.

White, with the fate of the colony in his hands, could do nothing. And after the defeat of the Spanish invasion attempt, he found that Raleigh had other things on his mind.

Raleigh's colonizing charter, which had been granted for six years, had almost run out. If, as he suspected, the Virginia settlers were all dead, he would lose his rights—and there was no hope of sending a new expedition in time. Raleigh was no longer interested in finding out whether the settlers were alive or not. So, in March, 1589, he leased his charter to the nineteen merchants who had financed the expedition of 1586, retaining the rights to one fifth of any gold or silver that might be discovered in Virginia. The group began at once to equip a

ship to send to the colony. But in February, 1590, after rumors of a second Armada, the ports were closed again.

White was in despair. He continued to harass Raleigh with pleas for help, and at last, Raleigh found a solution. He discovered that a merchant named John Watts wanted to send three merchant vessels to the West Indies. Raleigh promised to have the ban on Watts' ships lifted if the merchant would take the governor and a load of supplies to Roanoke Island.

The ships sailed in March, 1590, but they carried no relief for the colony. At the last moment, the crew of the *Hopewell*, on which the governor was traveling, refused to take aboard the supplies. And once the little fleet reached the West Indies, the captain spent several weeks privateering before turning north to Virginia. It was August before White sighted the string of islands rising off the Carolina coast: almost three years had passed since he had last seen them.

As soon as the *Hopewell* anchored off Roanoke, White insisted that a

Each of the battle charts opposite, published two years after the 1588 defeat of the Spanish Armada, depicts two separate actions. At top, English ships out of Plymouth attack the Spanish fleet, which then forms a tight circle to flee toward France. At bottom, English fireboats drive the Spaniards from their safe anchorage at the French port of Calais, and a final engagement is fought just off the coast.

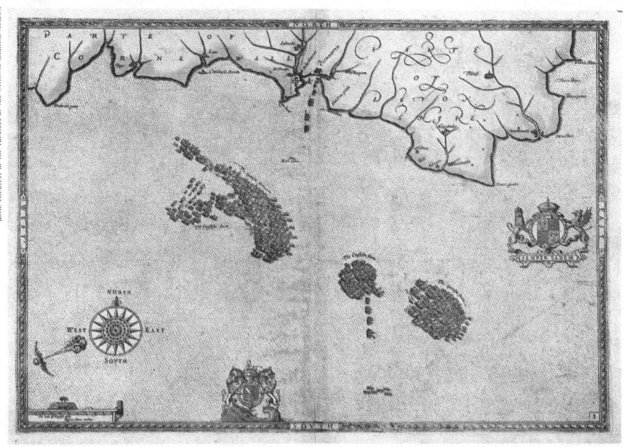

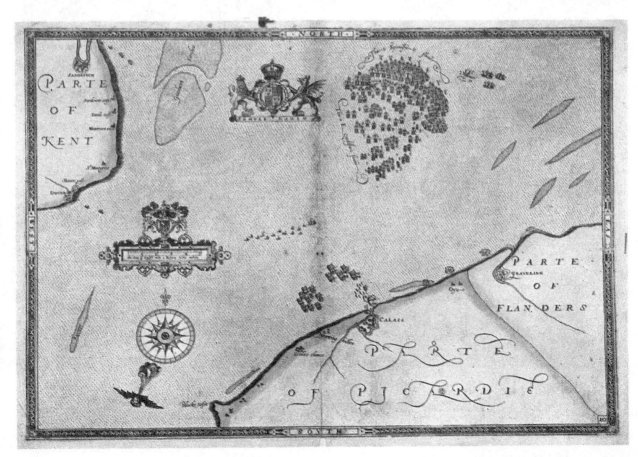

HISTORIC FORT RALEIGH

Most traces of Raleigh's 1585–87 colony on North Carolina's Roanoke Island had vanished within a few years of the mysterious disappearance of the settlers, but in 1950 the U.S. National Park Service reconstructed Ralph Lane's 1585 fort on its original site. In the aerial photograph at left the rebuilt fort is seen as a rough square, with two entrances on the right and pointed bastions at the left. Just inside the walls, which enclose an area about fifty feet square, is a raised fire ramp. The clay pipe and pots restored from fragments (below) indicate that Indians returned to the area after it had been abandoned by white men and perhaps lived amid the ruins.

The cautious and finicky James VI of Scotland became James I, king of England and Scotland, when Elizabeth I died in 1603.

search party go ashore, even though night was falling. Seeing a fire in the distance, one of the sailors sounded a trumpet call, and the rest sang at the top of their voices to attract attention.

On the morning of the following day, they headed for the site of the settlement. Silence greeted them. The fort was grass-grown and deserted. (The fire they had seen the night before was a brush fire, probably started by lightning.) In a nearby ditch, there were five broken chests, three of them belonging to White. He also found some of his books, which had been ripped from their covers, some of his maps, rotted and stained by the damp, and his armor, which was almost eaten through with rust. On one of the gateposts of the fort someone had carved the word "Croatoan." This was a sign, agreed upon before White had left, to show that the settlers had moved. (They were to have added a cross if they were in danger.) And since Croatoan Island was the home of Manteo's friendly tribe, White felt confident that the colony would be found in its new location.

He prepared to sail over to the island on the following day. But during the night, a fierce storm blew up. The *Hopewell* lost all but one anchor, and her captain, who was more concerned for his ship than for White's colonists, decided to run for safety in the West Indies. But once again the weather was against him. Howling gales blew the ship away from the coast and halfway across the Atlantic. He refused to try again, and a despondent White was taken back to England.

The second governor of Virginia was never to discover the fate of his daughter, his grandchild, or his comrades who had set out so bravely and hopefully in the spring of 1586. Although several search parties were sent out later, no clue to the settlers' fate was ever discovered on Croatoan Island or elsewhere. They passed into Virginia legend as the Lost Colony.

White himself made at least one

more attempt to find the Lost Colony, for he mentioned a fifth trip in a letter to Richard Hakluyt. Ironically, his own end is as obscure as that of the colonists. Where and when he died is unknown. But in 1606 his sister was made administrator of the will of a John White, "Late of parts beyond the sea," who must have been the same man. So, it seems likely, White died still looking for the men and women he had been unable to save.

Raleigh's end came in a blaze of publicity. When James I succeeded Elizabeth to the throne in 1603, the queen's old favorite fell from grace. James wanted peace with Spain, and he rightly saw Raleigh as a danger to his plans. Besides, the new monarch loathed the smoking habit, which he regarded as unhealthy, if not down-right sinful. And Raleigh had been responsible for making the habit of smoking Caribbean tobacco popular in England.

So, because of a mixture of high policy and personal dislike, Raleigh was flung into the Tower for treason. His titles, estates, and income were stripped from him, and his colonizing charter was given to others. He was finally released from the Tower in 1616 to make a vain attempt to find gold in Guiana for James. But, despite his promise to the king to avoid a clash with Spain, he tangled with the Spanish authorities, and when he returned to England, he paid for his error on the block.

In any case, the day of the lone promoter was over. The failure of the early colonies had made one thing clear: no effort could succeed without royal favor and businesslike planning. A new breed of men, middle-class merchants, were to profit from Raleigh's mistakes. To them must go the credit for planting England's first successful settlement in the New World.

Sir Walter Raleigh's well-attended execution is above. To James, Raleigh was a nuisance and a reminder of Elizabeth's glory.

3

JAMES FORT

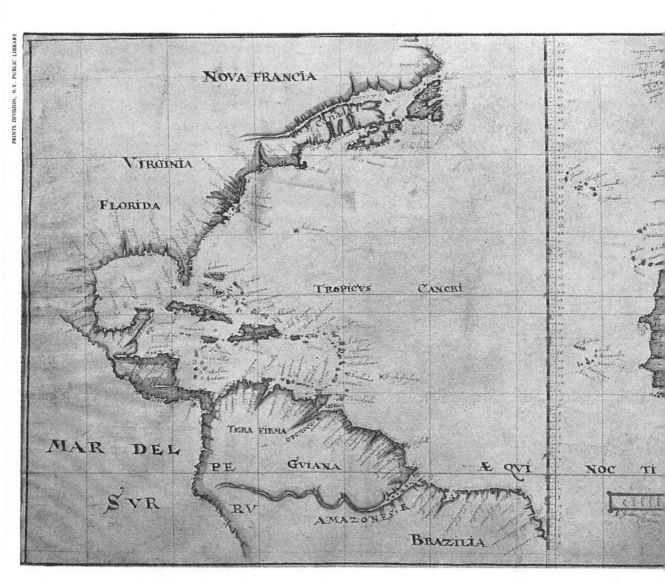

North America, in this map issued by the London Company about 1608, is divided among France (Nova Francia), England (Virginia), and Spain (Florida).

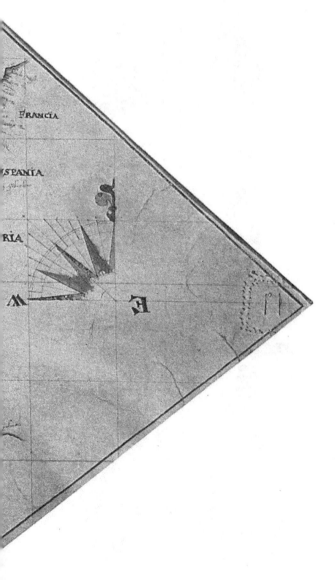

In 1606, three years after James I was crowned king of England, ten of the men who had backed White's expedition formed a company—the London Company—to colonize Virginia. For the most part they were well-to-do merchants, but their number also included Richard Hakluyt and a well-known liberal member of Parliament, Sir Edwin Sandys.

Sandys and three others petitioned James for a new royal charter, which was granted in the same year. The provisions of the new patent showed how much thought had been given to the question of planting a colony in the decade since Raleigh's last ill-fated attempt. Even Francis Bacon, soon to be Lord Chancellor of England, and one of the greatest minds of the age, had considered the problem of colonization.

Bacon decried the get-rich-quick motive: a colony, he argued, was a long-range scheme. Settlers had to be given twenty years to find their feet; they should expect to spend their lives in the colony; they should be selected for their special skills; and they should include many farmers, so that the colony could become self-sufficient.

Such far-sighted ideas influenced the makers of the new charter. It provided for a government in the colony consisting of a council of thirteen settlers, who would be directed by a royal council of thirteen in England. The colonial council would select one of its members as president of the New World colony and would make laws, vote taxes, mint money, and dispense justice in Virginia. Every settler would be granted "all liberties, franchises, and immunities . . ." of English citizens at home—which included the right to own land and the right of trial by jury. All taxes on trade with Virginia would be used for the benefit of the colony. This practical and liberal approach differed greatly from the fortune-hunting ideas that had characterized earlier overseas moves.

On December 20, 1606, the London Company's first expedition sailed from Blackwall, near London. Three ships, their holds crammed with tools, weapons, ammunition, food, and grain, made their way down the Thames with 105 hardy adventurers aboard. Many of them were classed as "gentlemen" in the ship's log, and in keeping with the new ideas, some others were skilled craftsmen and farmers. There were even two surgeons, one of whom was listed as a gentleman, the other not. And the colonists' reasons for risking their lives on this perilous voyage were almost as varied as their backgrounds. Some were the younger sons of noblemen, hoping to find in the New World the acres they could never hope to inherit from their fathers. Some had hopes of gold or quick fortunes in trade. Some sought a greater measure of liberty; some were merely restless; some were driven simply by the love of adventure. But they all shared a hope for better things in Virginia.

Aboard the flagship was a sealed

The sponsors of the Virginia colony hoped to attract settlers from all walks of life. Differences in rank, from nobleman to countryman, were reflected in the modes of dress.

box containing the names of the councilors along with the London Company's instructions, drawn up by the
king's council for Virginia. The instructions covered such down-to-earth
matters as the selection of a site for
the colony, notes on crops, and some
rules on how to deal with the Indians.
But more important, from the backers' point of view, were the three main
directions to the council. They were
to search for gold and other precious
metals; they were to explore the rivers
for a passage to the South Sea (the
Northwest Passage again); and they
were to look for the Lost Colony. New
ideas may have been introduced, but
old ones died hard.

The box was not to be opened
until the expedition reached Virginia.
Before then, the colonists would have
many hazards to face, for life aboard
ship in those days was cramped and
unhealthy. The largest of the London Company's vessels, The *Susan
Constant*, was fairly roomy, having
a displacement of one hundred tons.
But the *Godspeed* (forty tons) and
the *Discovery* (twenty tons) were
small and incommodious. In bad
weather it would be almost unbear-
able. The ships would be at sea for at
least four weeks before reaching the
West Indies, where fresh water, fruit,
and vegetables could be obtained; until then, food (for those who could
keep it down) would consist of little
more than rock-hard ship's biscuit,
saltmeat and fish, and barley gruel.

The new Virginia venture began

*English merchants who pressed the search
for new lands and encouraged colonization
formed into companies chartered by the
Crown. Above is the coat of arms of the
Merchant Adventurers, trading in Holland;
below, that of the East India Company.*

Griffith Baily Coale's painting in the Virginia State Capitol depicts the overcrowded ships God

speed, Susan Constant, *and* Discovery *(left to right) that brought English colonists to Jamestown.*

Photographs of the James River area as it looks today show (above) Archers Hope, a cove rejected as the colony site because of shallow water along the shore, and (right) Jamestown Island.

badly enough. The ships were unable to move from their anchorage off the coast of Kent for six weeks because of stormy weather. The chaplain, Robert Hunt, whose home was only twenty miles away, became so ill that it seemed he would die before he managed to get any nearer to his destination. Yet he rallied, and instead of complaining, urged his fellow sufferers to hang on.

Finally, in February of 1607, the wind changed, and the ships set sail. After taking on water at the Canary Islands, they steered westward on the long haul to the West Indies. They sighted Martinique on March 23. The travel-weary voyagers were allowed three weeks to recover from their or-

deal and to trade among the islands. But in early April, they were at sea again, making past Puerto Rico and landing on the tiny island of Mona. There they suffered their first casualty, a man named Edward Brooke. And on the nearby island of Monica, they found birds' eggs "as thick as drops of hail" and brought two boatloads back to the ships—a welcome addition to their shipboard fare.

On April 10, they weighed anchor and sailed north on the last leg of their journey. Eleven days later, they ran into a storm so violent that the captain of the *Discovery*, John Ratcliffe, almost put up his helm and turned for home. However, they believed they were within a few days' sail of their

BRY, *America*, PART X, 1619

This early version of the arrival at Jamestown includes a large, enthusiastic Indian reception committee. The map opposite, above, shows the route from London (1), to the Canary Islands (2), Martinique (3), and Mona Island off Puerto Rico (4). After sighting Virginia off Cape Henry (5), the ships sailed up the James (6) to Jamestown (7).

56

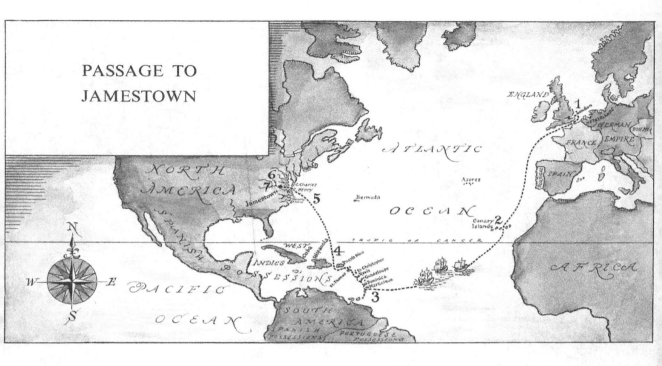

PASSAGE TO
JAMESTOWN

destination, and so they pressed on. On April 26, George Percy, one of the Earl of Northumberland's too-numerous sons, was able to record in his diary: "About four o'clock in the morning, we descried the land of Virginia."

The sight that greeted them was a reward for the perils of their long voyage. Unspoiled forests covered the land as far as the eye could see. Many of the trees were new to them—snake-wood, cedar, chinquapin, and sassa-fras. (These roots were later exported to England as an important item of trade.) The more familiar trees grew thicker and taller than they did at home, and no English spring could match the color of Virginia, ablaze

with dogwood, honeysuckle, and wild rose. Grapes and raspberries flourished everywhere, and in some places strawberries covered the ground so thickly that it was almost impossible to take a step without crushing them underfoot.

The woods teemed with game that spring, for the Indians did most of their hunting in the winter. Many of the animals were also new to the colonists: they had never seen an opossum, or a raccoon, which they thought was a kind of monkey at first, and they were amazed at the number and the tameness of the deer. The birds—white herons, red-headed woodpeckers, cardinals, and blackbirds—were brighter than the English species, and

This clearing near the shore of Jamestown Island looks much like descriptions of th

58

colonists' first assembly point.

wild turkeys and passenger pigeons, which they had not seen before, were to help tide the settlers over many a hungry winter.

After they had taken time to admire the abundance of their new home, the colonists settled down to business. First they opened the box of instructions put aboard in London. Seven of the thirteen councilors were named in these instructions; Captain Christopher Newport, the commander of the little fleet, and his two captains, John Ratcliffe and Bartholomew Gosnold, were first named. The other four were Edward Maria Wingfield, a Catholic gentleman, a seasoned soldier, and the only investor to make the trip; George Kendall and John Martin, both experienced mariners; and an unruly soldier of fortune named John Smith, who had spent most of the trip in irons for grumbling at the conduct of the officers on his ship.

A few days later, the council, in accordance with its instructions, elected its president—Edward Maria Wingfield.

The next task was to choose a site for the settlement. For that purpose an advance party was sent out to explore the country. When the explorers returned with a report of a great river stretching inland, the colonists prepared to move on. After giving thanks to God and erecting a cross on what they called Cape Henry (in honor of the eldest English prince), they hoisted sail and started up the James River (named in honor of their sovereign).

At one point they clashed with an Indian hunting party, and several of them, including Gabriel Archer, the secretary of the council, were wounded. But as they moved up the river, surveying both banks, they met nothing but friendliness. At each village they were entertained with banquets and dancing.

At last, on May 13, they found the site they had been looking for, some thirty miles upriver from Hampton Roads. It was a flat peninsula, nearly three miles long and from 300 to 2,000 yards wide, lying on the north side of the river. The only bridge to the mainland was a narrow isthmus that was covered at high tide, while on the river side of the peninsula the water was six fathoms deep. This meant that the ships could be brought up to the land and moored to the trees.

In some ways it was a good place

Corn, or maize, mainstay of the Indian diet

to settle. It could be defended with ease (fear of a sea raid by Spaniards loomed large in the colonists' minds), and there was a clear view down river to the sea. But there were also some serious drawbacks. The land was low and boggy, the sandy soil was poor, and deadly malaria mosquitoes bred in the swamps.

On May 14, the hundred-odd colonists and the council went ashore. After walking across the sand and up onto the bank, they gathered on the firm ground. The site would be called Jamestown (or James Fort), they decided, as a further honor to their sovereign. The venture that had begun in the time of the Elizabethan knights and that had been made possible by London businessmen was now in their hands.

Pumpkins, another leading Indian crop

Under the direction of John Smith, who had been released at the request of Captain Newport, the settlers began to build a log fort. Half of them were gentlemen who had never worked with their hands before, but the bushy-haired Smith drove every man to work with furious haste, and with good reason. With the fortification only half finished, the settlement was attacked by hostile Indians, who killed one boy and wounded eleven men before they were driven off by the ships' guns.

This mixed pattern of friendliness and enmity with neighboring tribes was to bedevil the colonists for decades. The Indians who lived in the surrounding territory belonged to a group governed by a powerful werowance, or high chief, named Powhatan.

Powhatan's people still lived in the Stone Age. They had never learned to smelt metals (copper pots that they later received from the white men were considered a great luxury and a mark of status); they had never even discovered the wheel. They built their swamp-grass huts in clearings near a river or stream. Each village was surrounded by fields where crops of corn, beans, squash, and tobacco were grown. The men cleared the ground, and both men and women farmed it. The men also hunted during the winter months with primitive hazel or locust-wood bows and arrows tipped with flint or bone. Fish were caught in dams of plaited reed or speared from dugout canoes, and the waters along

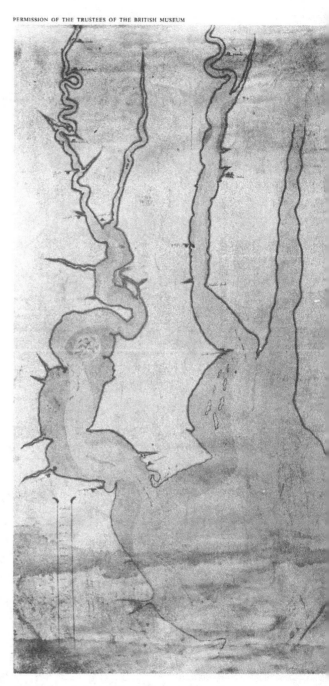

Colonist Robert Tindall drew the first map of the Virginia settlement in 1608, showing the James (left) and York rivers emptying into Chesapeake Bay (bottom). Jamestown (green dot) is above the James' first bend.

Above is an early view of Indians grilling fish. Below, two men trim the branches of a tree felled by fire (background) as two others work at burning and scraping the log into a canoe.

the shore yielded a harvest of shellfish.

War between the tribes was common; it was the usual way to settle disputes. Warriors painted themselves with red dyes and smeared their bodies with grease, and they were experts at ambush and surprise attacks. Skilled in woodsmanship and fighting from cover with their bows and at close quarters with clubs and stone tomahawks, the Indians were dangerous enemies, for they neither showed nor expected mercy.

Yet, though the Indians took their toll of colonists, the newcomers had even more deadly enemies to face. They found their water supply was salty, contaminated by the sea, which tided upriver, even beyond the settlement. And the disease-bearing mosquitoes were soon to begin devastating inroads on the colony.

Even so, as John Smith reported, the men stayed hard at work. "The council contrived the fort, the rest cut down trees to make place to pitch their tents; some provided clapboards to reload the ships, some made gardens, some nets . . ." The triangular fort, built of readily available timber, was 420 feet long facing the river and 300 feet long on the other two sides. At the corners were bulwarks with cannon mounted in them. In the enclosed area (about an acre), the colonists started to build crude houses, storage bins, and a church. On June 21, the third Sunday after Trinity, a piece of sail was stretched between two trees, and a rough altar was erected. There, communion was celebrated according to the rites of the English Church, the first recorded time in any overseas colony.

The next morning, Captain Newport set sail for England, planning to return soon with supplies. He took with him some stones veined with glittering metal that he hoped might be gold. The remaining colonists, equipped with three months' provisions, were left in Virginia to face the anxious wait.

Earlier, Newport, who was the most influential man on the council, had led an exploration party further up the river, following the London Company's instructions. At the falls, about fifty miles from Jamestown, they had found a fair-haired child living in an Indian village. The boy was thought to be the son of one of the survivors of the Lost Colony. Newport and his party had also visited Powhatan and had been feasted by him. After a week, Newport had returned, but he had found nothing to indicate that the James River might lead to the South Sea.

Before long, the settlers left at Jamestown found that the discomforts of the site could not be dispelled or ignored. The heat sapped their strength, and nearly all work came to a standstill. Brackish water, rotten food, and the climate brought dysentery, and the mosquitoes brought malaria. Miserable, irritable, and weak, the leaders began to quarrel. Small incidents festered, plots were hatched, petty disagreements became major disputes. Newport's skill as a peacemaker and his strength of character were sorely missed.

During that dreadful summer, colonists died by the score, including Captain Gosnold, probably of typhoid fever. Even reduced to five, the council was unable to work together. In September, Wingfield was overthrown by an alliance of Smith, Ratcliffe, and Martin. The charges against him were flimsy—he had allotted food and funds unfairly, he was an atheist, he was a Spanish spy—but in the strife-ridden atmosphere of Jamestown, these were enough.

Ratcliffe was elected president by his co-plotters, who soon found an opportunity to get rid of Kendall. A colonist on trial for striking the new president saved his own life by "confessing" that Kendall was plotting a rebellion. The three who had ousted Wingfield quickly brought their colleague to trial for mutiny and then executed him.

By December, the colony was in desperate straits. Living in mere huts, their food running low, their leadership divided and unable to keep discipline, and constantly threatened by the Indians, the colonists seemed doomed to the same fate that had overtaken their predecessors. But as sometimes happens in human affairs, the hour found a man to match it. John Smith had begun his life in the colony in disgrace; now he was to emerge as its savior.

With their three ships anchored in the James River, the Jamestown settlers turned to their first task, building a triangular palisade to protect the tiny settlement against Indian attack.

4

THE GOLDEN LEAF

The Chickahominy is a peaceful little river ninety miles long that empties into the James ten miles above Jamestown. But to Captain John Smith—who had already demonstrated that he was the boldest and most imaginative of the fifty-odd colonists who still survived at Jamestown—the Chickahominy seemed to offer a fair promise of leading directly to the heart of the New World. And perhaps if he reached the source of the river, he would discover gold mines or spy the South Sea beyond the crest. Yet, perhaps this river too would merely bring more disappointment, leading only, like the James itself, to waterfalls and a wilderness of mountain ridges.

With the resolve that he must find something up the Chickahominy to sustain life and hope in the colony (even if it were only a supply of Indian corn to fill their empty larders), Smith set out with a small party of men in a boat on December 10, 1607. All too soon the waterway began to narrow; when the trees on the banks overgrew the river, even Smith saw that going farther was pointless. After leaving their craft, with men to guard

it, and continuing a way with an Indian guide, they were fiercely attacked by a band of savages. John Smith, who had faced danger in battle many times before coming to Virginia, undoubtedly put up a strong defense. Never in his life had he been shy about using his sword.

Born in 1580, he soon proved himself a poor scholar and had run off to sea at sixteen. Then there followed years of military adventures in Europe, all of which (both the true and the almost true) he described in his later writings. Having invested most of his booty in the London Company, he had come to the colony at the age of twenty-seven both for adventure and to improve his fortunes. Now, with the tide of battle running against him, it looked as if the young soldier might lose all. Smith's two companions fell before the Indians' furious assault, and at last the captain him-

The published works of John Smith are full of vigorous illustrations like the one opposite, which shows the sturdy captain grasping Opechancanough by the hair in 1608.

C Smith taketh the King of Pamavnkee prisoner 1608

His Combat with GRVALGO. Cap.t of threehundred horsmen.
Chap. 7.

self was captured as the Indians made a final assault.

The braves who presented Smith to their chief were Pamunkeys, one of the many tribes in the Powhatan Confederation, and their chief was one of Powhatan's most powerful allies. His name was Opechancanough—a name the colonists would later have reason to hear with dread.

At first the Pamunkeys were inclined to kill Smith outright, but the bold Englishman had the wit to keep talking. Taking his compass from his pocket, he fascinated his captors by showing them how the tiny needle always pointed in the same direction.

Smith had killed three Turks in single combat during his European campaigns (above); thus he was given a coat of arms with three turbaned heads (below). That distinction was of little help up the Chickahominy, when he tried to ward off his Indian attackers by using his guide as a shield (opposite). He was captured only after falling into a swamp.

They tried to touch the needle and stop its swinging but could not because of the glass. All the while Smith kept talking on, with grand gestures, about the wonders of the universe. And by the time the uncomprehended lecture was finished, the Pamunkeys had concluded that the great white warrior, whether mad or inspired, was surely a rare prize.

They allowed Smith to send a message back to Jamestown telling of his capture. Then they took him to Werowacomoco, the main village of Chief Powhatan, on the north side of what is now called the York River. The chief summarily condemned him for having killed two Indians in the battle at the head of the Chickahominy. Preparations were begun to execute Smith in the traditional manner—placing his head on a rock and beating his brains out with a club.

What saved Smith this time was his good looks—or so it would appear from his own account, written later. Up ran Powhatan's twelve-year-old daughter Matoaka, whose nickname Pocahontas meant "lively one." She took Smith's head in her arms, indicating that he was to be spared and that she would be responsible for him.

Although John Smith could not know that his salvation (and virtual adoption) by the chief's daughter would mean the establishment of a period of peace between the settlers and the Powhatan Confederation, he could and did express his gratitude. With his customary persuasiveness he told the chief that the English had come to trade and explore, not to take the Indians' land. And he ended by making a successful plea for corn.

Thus, when Smith returned to the fort at Jamestown on January 2, 1608,

SMITH, Generall Historie of Virginia, 1624

Ætatis suæ 21. Aº 1616.

This appealing portrait of Princess Pocahontas in a tall hat and English dress was painted in London when she was twenty-one—nine years after she had saved the life of John Smith.

he expected to be greeted warmly, both for the corn he brought and for his tidings of peace. Instead he was seized and bound, and once more he was imprisoned. None of this was deserved. Gabriel Archer, a cunning lawyer and Smith's determined opponent, had been admitted to the council during Smith's absence and had been able to influence its members against the strong-minded captain. When word came that two of Smith's men had been killed on the expedition up the Chickahominy, Archer had persuaded the councilors that Smith should be held accountable.

There was an immediate trial, and Smith was convicted. But again fortune came to his rescue. The sails of an English ship were spotted coming up the James River. Commanding the ship was Captain Newport, whose arrival had been expected for several weeks. Sizing up the situation, Newport brought about Smith's release. He also recognized Smith's great accomplishment among the Indians, and a few weeks later he arranged to visit Powhatan himself.

The arrival of Newport and the so-called first supply was, along with later supplies, the vital lifeline that kept the colony from perishing. He brought food, arms, and more settlers. He also reported to the council that the London Company's desire for gold had been made no less keen by the discovery that the ore he had taken back with him was worthless.

After Newport departed for England in the spring (taking Archer, Wingfield, and Martin), Smith set out on a major expedition up Chesapeake Bay. He saw to it before leaving that the ravages of a winter fire were repaired and that some acreage immediately outside the fort was cultivated, but he knew that the outpost was still unstable and insecure.

The purpose of the Chesapeake survey, as Smith later wrote was ". . . to search a glittering metal the savages told us they had from Patawomeck [Potomac] . . . also to search what furs, metals, rivers, rocks, nations, woods, fishings, fruits, victuals, and other commodities the land afforded; and whether the bay were endless, or how far it extended." On this voyage Smith found the Potomac River and was attacked by a sting ray while "stabbing fish" with his sword. He feared that he would die as a result of the episode. Later, when he made his wonderfully accurate 1612 map of Virginia, he gave a prominent label to "Stingra Ile."

Despite such adventures, the trip produced neither gold nor visions of a southern sea, and when Smith returned he found that the colony was again in a political uproar. But in the absence of Archer and Martin, the twenty-nine-year-old leader was able to effect the deposition of President Ratcliffe. Smith was then elected to the presidency of the colony and was able to enforce a measure of discipline among the contentious colonists.

At this fortunate moment, early in

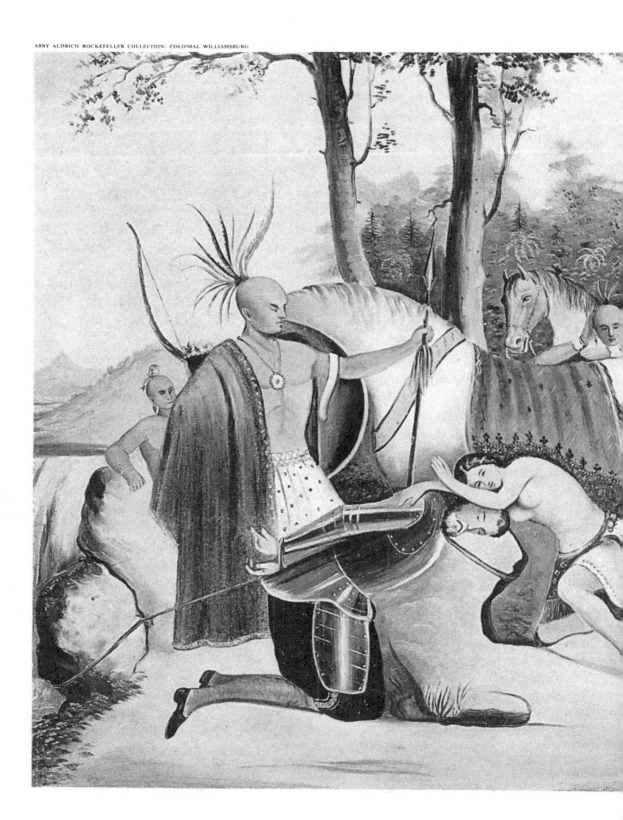

October of 1608, Captain Newport arrived with the second supply. It was a mixed bag of seventy passengers and worrisome presentiments that he brought. As well as eight Germans and Poles who were to set up a glassworks, plus two women (the colony's first), he bore a number of unreasonable demands from the London Company. It asked, of course, that the colonists continue to search for the elusive gold mines and discover the way to the East Indies. The company had also made Newport swear he would return with a cargo of sufficient value to pay for his voyage.

John Smith, convinced by this time that he knew more about colonizing than the gentlemen in London, and angered by the company's demands, issued what has become known as the Rude Reply. Referring to the ill-provisioned and mostly unskilled passengers who arrived with Newport, he wrote: "When you send again I entreat you rather send but thirty carpenters, husbandmen, gardeners, fishermen, blacksmiths, masons, and diggers up of trees' roots, well-provided, than a thousand of such as we have. For except we be able to lodge and feed them, most will consume with want of necessaries before they can be made good for anything."

An unknown American artist created this vivid re-enactment of Pocahontas' famous deed. Though the episode has the sound of a myth, many accept it as a historical fact.

73

Of all Smith's contributions to the colony, perhaps the two greatest were the peace he made with the Indians of the Powhatan Confederation and the mapping he did of the great rivers. The portion of his 1612 map reproduced above is the James River valley. The "X" marks indicate the farthest extent of Smith's own investigations. Set into the map is a drawing of Powhatan in his lodge.

Despite these grumblings, Smith was doing well with what he had. Fields were cleared, and Indian hostages showed the colonists how to plant corn in hills. To defend against any Indians who might remain hostile, a blockhouse was built at the point where the Jamestown peninsula narrowed down to the sand isthmus that extended to the mainland. In the James River on an island henceforth called Hog Island an outpost was established. A number of pigs were taken to the island where they could freely roam and multiply. "Of three sows in eighteen months, increased more than sixty pigs," Smith recorded. "And nearly five hundred chickens brought up themselves without care."

Everywhere there were signs of growth. Smith commanded and sometimes bullied the men under him. He made them learn military drill and stand watch, and otherwise played the one-time officer. His efforts were rewarded with peace and a promise of abundance.

Leaving behind him some two hundred healthy colonists (one pair of whom—Anne Burras and John Laydon—were soon married), and taking with him a cargo of pitch, iron ore, and glass, plus Smith's reply, Newport sailed for England at the end of 1608. He also took with him the disgraced former president of the colony, John Ratcliffe. Unfortunately, a series of mishaps struck the colony soon after his pennants had disap-

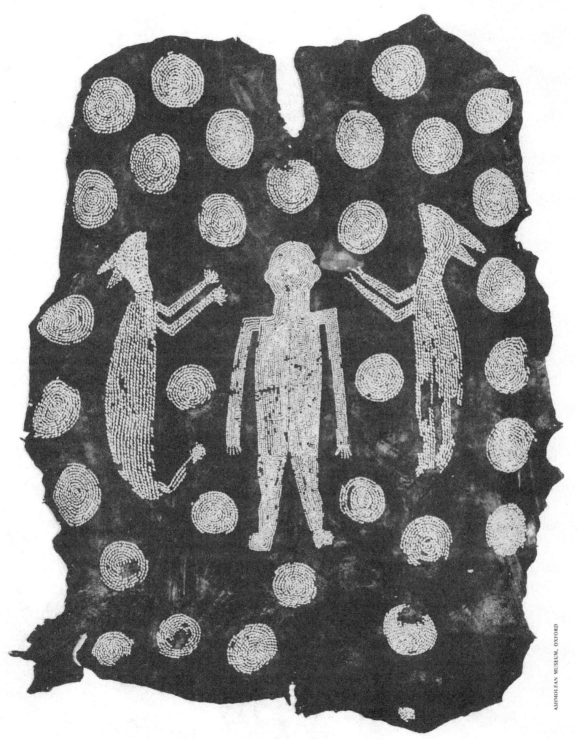

This deerskin decorated with figures made of shells is said to have been Powhatan's ceremonial cloak. It was taken to England in the 1600's.

Settlers and savages congregate on the beach in John Gadsby Chapman's 1841 painting entitled "Land-ing at Jamestown, 1608-1609." The landing referred to is most probably the arrival of Captain New-

port's second supply in 1608—note the two women passengers (at left of center). Without Newport's skill in crossing the Atlantic with more settlers and goods, the colony might have perished.

peared over the horizon. The first was the discovery that rats had invaded the Jamestown storehouse; half the grain supply had been eaten or was rotten. Smith, now that his leadership was unchallenged, immediately came forward with a plan: some of the two hundred colonists were sent to fish at Point Comfort; some went to live with the Indians; others were dispatched to gather oysters down the James and in Chesapeake Bay.

The plan worked, but John Smith had more difficulty coping with the second crisis that struck Jamestown after Newport's departure. In August, 1609, seven ships of the third supply came straggling in from the sea. Two of them were so battered by a hurricane that they no longer had mainmasts; of two others that had left London in June, one was known to have gone to the bottom, and the second, the *Sea Venture*, was believed to have been wrecked in the Bermudas. Worse still, the ships that did reach Virginia carried with them some two or three hundred dying or ailing Englishmen—many of the sick, when healthy, were loafers and renegades. The colony simply could not accommodate so many mouths; mass starvation began to loom as a possibility.

Among these miserable arrivals were three former council members. John Martin, John Ratcliffe, and (like the proverbial bad penny) Gabriel Archer. They were quick to tell Smith of a new charter the company had drafted, and they were even more eager to point out that this meant his administration was no longer valid. Smith could argue that since all of the papers they referred to had been lost with the ship wrecked in the Bermudas, their claim had little validity either. At length a compromise was reached: Smith would finish out his term as president, but the three newcomers would dominate the council.

Thus, when the third crisis came in late September, Smith was already in the shadow of his enemies. He had gone on one of his expeditions—this time more than one hundred miles up the James, beyond the falls—and once again had returned without news of any astonishing discoveries. Even worse, he had also returned with a serious wound in his thigh, which had resulted from an unexplained gunpowder explosion. Incapacitated, and confronted by his old enemies, Smith was for once unable to prevail. He was hustled aboard the first ship leaving Jamestown, summarily dispatched to England for "proper medical treatment."

Although John Smith was taken away from Virginia after only two years' service there, he had already demonstrated such high qualities of leadership that it can be said he was almost solely responsible for the colony's initial survival. It was he who kept up the morale of the small group of settlers who survived the first winter; it was he who was able to obtain corn and other supplies from the Indians; and it was he who commanded

An English artist entranced by the drawings of John White and by descriptions of Virginia's wildlife was Edward Topsell (1572–1625). His paintings of a red-winged blackbird and an Eastern bluebird are at left.

By the time of John Smith's departure, the one acre in James Fort was crowded—with a church (at center in the reconstructed view below), a storehouse (at right of well), and many thatched houses. For the first time, fields beyond the walls were being cleared and planted; the wilderness was retreating.

79

All too many of the passengers on the first supplies had had a brush with the jailer. The fellow in the seventeenth-century woodcut above, hauled to jail by pikemen, is apparently giving the warden his possessions —to the amusement of street musicians.

sufficient personal authority to impose necessary discipline on the colonists. He would never again see Virginia—the spot he called "my wife, to whom I have given all." But he was able to support the cause of the colony with his pen. While still in the colony he had written a colorful account of Jamestown's settlement and survival called *A True Relation of . . . Virginia Since the First Planting of That Colony* (published in London in 1608). And before his death in 1631 he was able to complete his *Generall Historie of Virginia. . .* and *The True Travels, Adventures, and Observations of Captaine John Smith . . .* both of which helped attract new waves of immigrants to the New World colony which he had so valiantly defended.

An earlier document drafted by Smith, his Rude Reply, had results of another kind. It helped the London Company see that a far larger effort had to be made, in terms of both men and material, in order to put the colony on a firm foundation. More money, and then more money, would be needed before returns (probably in the form of crops and raw materials rather than gold or spices) could be

England's honest and industrious yeomen farmers were recruited by the London Company to take part in the faltering New World experiment. The yeomen above are planting and grafting trees, using shovels and picks and sickles that still look familiar today.

expected. Thus, in 1609, the company was made a public corporation, and stock was sold to anyone who would buy. Fortunately, many did.

The company also took note of the political squabbles that had plagued Smith; obviously firmer direction of the council would have to be supplied from London. Thus, a new charter was prepared that allowed the directors to put Virginia's government in the hands of an omnipotent governor; the Virginia council was for the time being reduced to the status of an advisory body. This provision and other farsighted features of the 1609 charter were the work of Sir Edwin Sandys, the member of the company who remained most zealously devoted to the colonists' welfare.

Named to the all-powerful position of governor for life was Thomas West, Lord Delaware. It was Delaware who had organized the great expedition of the summer of 1609, the remnants of which had arrived in the colony in such bad shape before Smith's departure. It was the expedition's flagship, the *Sea Venture*, that had been blown onto the reefs of Bermuda (an incident immortalized

The Sea Venture, *flagship of the 1609 fleet, runs against the reefs of the Bermuda Islands. A boat bearing survivors pulls away from the battered wreck.*

in Shakespeare's play *The Tempest*). There, the survivors—including Lieutenant Governor Thomas Gates, Admiral George Somers, and a young gentleman named John Rolfe—were to spend many months trying to construct two small ships that could carry them to Virginia.

Delaware himself stayed in London until the following spring, gathering another, smaller, fleet. He acted swiftly, for he had heard of the wreck of the *Sea Venture*. He would have acted even more swiftly had he known of conditions in the colony.

As it happened, the winter of 1609-10—called the Starving Time—was the grimmest yet in Virginia's short and tragic history. The great number of settlers who had recently arrived imposed an impossible strain on the food supply. Without Smith's firm hand, discipline broke down, and relations with the Indians deteriorated. One group of thirty hungry colonists, led by Ratcliffe, was massacred by the Indians while bartering for food. Forced back into the fort, the weakened settlers were struck again and again by crippling and killing diseases.

Those who could, and who dared, crawled out through the fort's unguarded gates to catch snakes or dig up roots. Those who stayed in their huts died and were piled unceremoniously into common graves. Of the almost five hundred people in Virginia when Smith left in 1609, only sixty-five were alive six months later.

On May 23, 1610, relief appeared —in the form of two small ships that sailed slowly into view and into the Jamestown anchorage. Amid cries of joy the skeletonlike colonists learned that the newcomers were the survivors of the *Sea Venture*, who had succeeded in making their way from the Bermudas. Lieutenant Governor Gates, seeing the miserable condition of the settlement, and hearing of the Indians' hostility, realized that there was no possibility of staying there. So, after two weeks of additional repairs to his patchwork vessels, he ordered every man "at the beating of a drum to repair aboard." Thinking now only of England, the colonists set sail on June 7. Lacking wind, the ships anchored for the night a few

miles downstream off Hog Island. The following day a sail was seen in the distance. It proved to be that of a small boat sent ahead with a message for the colonists: three well-equipped ships were en route to Jamestown and had already passed Old Point Comfort; on board one ship was Lord Delaware, the new governor. Despite the "groans, curses, and great grief" of the bone-tired survivors, Gates turned his little ships back and moved up-river to Jamestown.

On June 10, 1610, Lord Delaware stepped from his ship at Jamestown, knelt, and thanked God that he had come in time to save the colony. A sermon of thanksgiving was preached. New laws were quickly put into effect in accordance with the 1609 charter,

In the grim illustration at left, a small burial party passes through the fort's gate in the desperate winter of 1609–10. By the time Gates and Lord Delaware (above) arrived, the colony was nearly starved out.

and discipline and order were restored. Bells were rung for prayers at
10:00 A.M. and 4:00 P.M. every day.
To avoid a repetition of the winter
disasters, strict laws were posted. For
pilfering food a colonist could have
his ears cut off; for repeating the crime,
he could be condemned to service as a
galley slave.

However, Governor Delaware, for
all his strength and wisdom, was not
fated to be the leader who finally succeeded in putting the colony on a firm
footing. Nor was Sir Thomas Gates,
who ruled as lieutenant governor from
1611 to 1614. Under this old soldier
the colony expanded greatly beyond
its palisaded confines. The first new
communities were established on the
mainland (notably Henrico Corporation), and at last the specter of starvation was banished.

Yet it was not in the person of a
military or political leader that true
prosperity at last came to Virginia; it
was in the person of an imaginative
planter. John Rolfe, the young man
who had made the crossing from the
Bermudas, began simple experiments
with a native tobacco weed (known
botanically as *Nicotiana rustica*) in the
spring of 1612, mostly for his own
use. He had heard that the Indians
occasionally smoked it or scattered it
to the winds as a part of a social or
religious ceremony. And he began to
wonder whether he could find a strain
better than this tobacco, which seemed
too harsh and too strong for civilized
tastes. He knew that tobacco imported

SIR RONALD LECHMERE

VIRGINIA STATE LIBRARY

Sir Thomas Dale cuts a fine military figure in the portrait opposite at bottom. As Marshall of Virginia under Gates, he earned a reputation for harsh discipline, although tortures like those above (burning, breaking on the wheel) were probably beyond him. Above Dale is Sir Edwin Sandys, who, unlike Dale, believed that the colonists should have a reasonable government.

by the Spaniards from the West Indies had become popular in Europe and even in England, where the king disapproved of the habit that Sir Walter Raleigh had popularized in 1586. Through a sea captain who sailed often to the Caribbean, Rolfe was able to obtain seeds of a broader-leaf tobacco plant (*Nicotiana tabacum*)—and thus began his further experiments with the golden leaf that would eventually support the colony's entire economy.

In June, 1613, the first shipment of Rolfe's tobacco was sent off to England. Just two months previously the young widower was one of the many colonists who learned to their astonishment that Captain Samuel Argall's ship *Treasurer*, anchored at Jamestown, held in its cabins none other than Pocahontas, the princess who had saved John Smith's life. Argall, trading up the Potomac River, had discovered that Pocahontas was staying with a local chieftain. He had kidnapped her after first buying the cooperation of the Indian ruler with a

Capit.Argal

The abductor of Pocahontas, Captain Samuel Argall, is seated amid a circle of Indians in the scene opposite by Theodore De Bry, the seventeenth-century Flemish engraver. Below that is another De Bry engraving showing Pocahontas (central figure in foreground) with the Indian chief and his wife who betrayed her to Argall. More sentimental is the nineteenth-century view at right of the baptism of "Rebecca" in 1613.

copper kettle and other simple inducements. The plan of the unscrupulous Argall was to hold Pocahontas as a hostage to insure better dealings for the colonists among the Indians. Lieutenant Governor Gates fell in with the plan, though he vowed the girl would be well treated. He proposed that she be educated and instructed in Christianity at Henrico, one of the colony's new settlements up the James.

It happened that Rolfe's plantation was also near Henrico, so he had a chance to observe Pocahontas and talk with her. During the course of these months he fell in love with the comely and lively girl. And he was doubtless present when she was brought to Jamestown to be baptized with the name Rebecca. In April of the following year (1614), the princess

and the planter were married, with the approval of Powhatan. The great chief vowed that there would be everlasting peace between the tribes of his confederation and the English colonists.

As John Rolfe's personal life flourished, so did his plantation. He found that the milder West Indian leaf was perfectly adaptable to Virginia's climate. Other settlers followed him in planting the tiny seeds, and in that year of 1615, 2,300 pounds of tobacco were shipped to England for profitable sale. Some aspects of tobacco cultivation were found to be potentially troublesome—it tended to exhaust the land in which it was grown, and many hands were needed to tend the fields— but these were given scant attention. Even more tobacco was exported the following year.

In 1616 Mr. and Mrs. Rolfe and

their infant son sailed for London, accompanied by an Indian retinue. Pocahontas was presented at court by Lady Delaware (whose husband held the title of governor until his death in 1618). She also had the pleasure of meeting Sir Walter Raleigh, who had been released from the Tower, and of re-meeting John Smith. Presumably she was also introduced to Sir Edwin Sandys (author in 1612 of a new charter for Virginia) and the other important members of the London Company. She made a most favorable impression in all these circles. But Pocahontas had the misfortune to contract smallpox early in 1617. She died in March, just before she and her husband were to take ship for Virginia.

COLONIAL WILLIAMSBURG

In the eighteenth-century drawings above, tobacco plants are set out and cured. For such labor strong backs and agile hands were needed. By the late 1600's scenes like that below—Negro laborers being delivered to a plantation—were no longer uncommon.

PRINTS DIVISION, N.Y. PUBLIC LIBRARY

The widowed John Rolfe arrived in Jamestown to find tobacco growing in "the marketplace, the streets, and all other spare places." The colony was enjoying its first economic boom: in 1617, 20,000 pounds were exported; in a decade that figure would be multiplied more than twenty-fold.

And as the tobacco fields extended outward from the settlements along the James, new colonists (mostly indentured servants) were welcomed with increased enthusiasm. In 1612, the colony's population passed the thousand mark; in 1619 alone, 1,261 immigrants arrived. (And just one year later a small band of Pilgrims set sail from England, bound for the northern part of Virginia and ended by founding the Plymouth Colony.)

By accident, twenty of the new arrivals at Jamestown were Negroes delivered to the colony by a buccaneer who had taken them in the West Indies. At first the Negroes were treated as indentured servants; only later did they become slaves.

Within a year of the Negroes' arrival came an even more wondrous shipment—a group of girls whose passage was paid by settlers. The social and economic life of the colony was growing—growing in patterns peculiar to the strange new world of the golden leaf.

As visualized by the American illustrator Howard Pyle, "The Arrival of the Brides at Jamestown in 1619" was a gay affair, with gentlemen and ladies dressed to the nines.

JAMESTOWN RECONSTRUCTED

A few overgrown ruins are all that remain today of
early Jamestown; the James River has even washed
away part of the original site and turned the peninsula into an island. But on the mainland, visitors can
see authentic reproductions of some of the early
buildings. In the thatch-roofed glasshouse (right), a
replica of what may be called America's first factory,
modern craftsmen give demonstrations of colonial
glass-blowing techniques. Nearby is Festival Park,
built in 1957 to commemorate the three hundred
and fiftieth anniversary of Jamestown's founding.
A veil of mist, like that which made the swampy site
an unhealthy place to live, hangs over reconstructed
James Fort (below) with its prisoners' stocks. Jamestown church (right, below) is a humble chapel.

93

Nova Britannia:

OFFERING MOST

Excellent fruites by Planting in
Virginia.

Exciting all such as be well affected
to further the same.

LONDON
Printed for S A M V E L   M A C H A M, and are to be sold at
his Shop in Pauls Church-yard, at the
Signe of the Bul-head.
1 6 0 9.

5

MASSACRE

Through the doors of the Jamestown church on July 30, 1619, walked one of the most hopeful groups of men ever to meet on this continent, the General Assembly of the Virginia Colony. First, wearing a plume in his hat and a sword at his side, came the new governor, Sir George Yeardley, a seasoned colonist who had already served a year as acting governor during the lifelong tenure of Lord Delaware. Now, with the death of Delaware in 1618, Sir George was in Jamestown to establish his own administration along the lines so carefully laid down by the London Company.

Then came the governor's six councilors, one of whom was John Rolfe. These gentlemen filled up the choir of the church and then waited silently while the movable pews were occupied by twenty-two newcomers to the affairs of state, men who were

Through the first two decades of the Virginia settlement, London backers continued to promote colonization with pamphlets that painted a rosy picture of New World life.

called burgesses. Two burgesses had been elected by the male adults of each of the colony's seven "particular" plantations (that is, the large development areas deeded by the company to a few favored investors); the remaining eight burgesses, elected in the same way, represented the four "general" plantations (areas for open settlement). As the delegates shuffled into their places none of them— whether members of the Council of State or of the House of Burgesses— removed their hats. For if the members of England's Parliament sat hatted, so, they felt, should they.

After listening to the opening prayers and taking oaths of allegiance to James I, the members accepted "with general assent and the applause of the whole assembly" the charter of 1612. This, as well as Governor Yeardley's own instructions, had been drafted by Sir Edwin Sandys with a fine eye to the best way to make the settlers work together and so put the colony on its feet. Thus representative democracy, in the form of the House of Burgesses, had come to the shores of America not as the gift of a king but as the policy of a far-sighted corporation.

It was taken for granted that the assembly had the power to levy taxes (in the form of tobacco) on the colonists for the support of the church and to pay for the assembly's meetings. But specific legislation was drafted, always according to the company's plans, to regulate such public matters as morality, land patents, foreign trade, tobacco prices, and the relationships between the landowners and their servants.

Three years previously, a land policy had been adopted that gave one hundred acres to each settler who had come to the colony before 1616. Thus, immigration was stimulated, and the "ancient planters," as that earlier generation was called, were encouraged to lay out large farms. Those who paid their own way and arrived in Jamestown after 1616 were given fifty acres for themselves, plus fifty more for each person whose passage they paid—whether a relative or an indentured servant.

Many of the indentured servants were solid yeomen or the younger sons of gentlemen, but many others were petty criminals or London riff-raff. Whatever their origins, they had all signed contracts agreeing to sell their services for four to seven years to pay for their passage to the New World. If they survived the crossing and the frightful diseases that consistently decimated the newly arrived workers, and when their term of serv-

96

The narrow room at Westminster pictured in the seventeenth-century engraving above is jammed with members of the English Parliament. This ancient body, which traced its origins back to the 1200's, became the model for the Virginia General Assembly. The assembly's first meeting is seen opposite in a painting by the modern artist Elmo Jones: light streams in through the windows of the little Jamestown church onto the councilors (background) and the burgesses (foreground). Above that illustration is the original report of the assembly, with a partial list of the twenty-two men (two from each district) who hoped to be installed as burgesses.

By 1619, Jamestown's colonists were feeling secure enough from Indian attack to build their houses outside the palisaded fort they had built on the James River's banks (background

This view of settlers bargaining at the central market place, rough clapboard houses (left) beginning to replace the daub and wattle structures (right) that were the first dwellings.

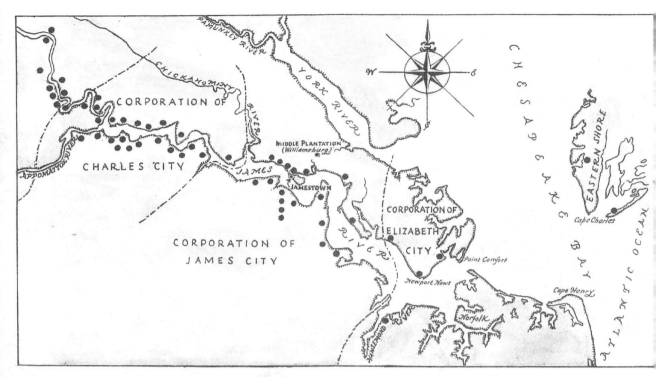

In the 1622 map of Virginia above, dotted lines indicate the boundaries between counties (corporations), while the dots represent the individual settlements. The iron foundry established after 1619 at the falls of the James River is shown by the uppermost dot at left. The 1622 broadside opposite, above, blames the previous hard times in Virginia on insufficient preparation by early colonists and includes a list of clothing, food, arms, tools, and household items that prospective settlers should take with them. The cost of such outfitting came to twenty pounds, the amount given to would-be colonists by the London Company. To those who could pay their way, the company promised fifty free acres. When bad news from Virginia reduced investment there, lotteries (right) were held in London to raise additional funds.

A Declaration for the certaine

THE INCONVENIENCIES
THAT HAVE HAPPENED TO SOME PER-
SONS WHICH HAVE TRANSPORTED THEMSELVES
from *England* to *Virginia*, without provisions necessary to sustaine themselves, hath
greatly hindred the Progresse of that noble Plantation: For prevention of the like disorders
hereafter, that no man suffer, either through ignorance or misinformation; it is thought re-
quisite to publish this short declaration: wherein is contained a particular of such necef-
faries, as either private families or single persons shall have cause to furnish themselves with,
for their better support at their first landing in Virginia; whereby also greater numbers may receive in part,
directions how to provide themselves.

Imprinted at London by FELIX KYNGSTON. 1622.

Copy 5

ing the great standing Lottery.

Matahan.

Il.
500

Deere *Britaines*, now, be *Ten* as kinde:
Bring *Light*, and *Sight*, to *Vs* yet blinde:
Leade *Vs*, by *Doctrine* and *Behaviour*,
Into one *Sion*, to one *SAVIOVR*.

uenture twelue pounds ten shillings or vpward, if he
please to leaue & remit his Prizes or Rewards, bee
they more or lesse, the Lottery being drawne out, hee
shall haue a bill of Aduenture to Virginia, for the like
summe he aduentured, & shall be free of that Company, &
haue his part in Lands, & all other profits hereafter
arising there, according to his aduenture of twelue
pounds ten shillings or vpwards.

Whosoeuer is behinde with the payment of any sum
of money, promised heretofore to be aduentured to Virginia, if hee aduenture in this Lotterie the double of

---

ice was up, they were given "freedom dues"—in the form of shoes, three barrels of corn, farming tools, and sometimes land. Then they were allowed to start planting on their own. The biggest problem at that point was not for them to find free acreage but to procure more indentured servants to work it.

Indeed, the whole democratic and growing economy of the colony was based on the availability of much land and the continuing immigration of many new hands. In the early decades, approximately two thirds of the colony's population arrived as servants —servants who expected soon to be masters.

As well as taking steps to control these social relationships and to protect the infant tobacco industry, the assembly encouraged the colonists to diversify their crops. The company had long feared that the colonists' inclination to plant nothing but tobacco and to rely on the Indians for corn and other foods was too risky. Now the assembly required that each planter put in ten wild grapevines a year (to make wine), a hundred flax plants (for linen), and six mulberry trees (whose leaves would feed silkworms).

Hopes that Jamestown might be made into a self-sustaining colony were revived: in 1610 "lymeburners" had been sent to the colony to try to convert James River oyster shells into lime to make mortar; efforts had also been made to manufacture bricks. Now, in 1619, 150 workers brought from England were dispatched sixty-six miles up the James to set up an iron foundry at Falling Creek, where excellent ore had been discovered by Captain Newport. In addition, attempts were made to produce pottery, tile, and potash. Yet Virginia remained overwhelmingly agricultural in its character and its outlook; it was a farmer state of fundamentally free and equal men.

Among the last acts of the councilors and the burgesses before they adjourned their historic first session was to decree (according to a suggestion of the company's) that each plantation be located ten miles from its nearest neighbor. Although Governor Yeardley had some reservations about this proposal, recognizing that it would space the colonists so widely that mutual defense against the Indians would be difficult, most of the planters considered the provision wise since it protected them from encroachment by their neighbors. The plantations were developing as little worlds unto themselves: they produced their own food; raised enough tobacco to require that ships from England and Holland stop at their separate wharves; and created a gentlemanly way of life that reflected English origins while also seeming an integral part of the new countryside.

The colonists believed that in the peaceful times they had been enjoying since Pocahontas' marriage to John Rolfe, the Indians would tolerate further and further extensions of the English plantations. Trade with the Indians was cautiously pursued as one means by which good relations might be maintained, though selling iron

Many of the early Virginia tobacco plantations had their own river wharves. In the old engraving above, slaves pack tobacco for shipment to England. The mantle painting below, made about 1700, depicts a river scene in Virginia, with an elaborate plantation house at right.

tools, or even dogs, to the natives was forbidden. In addition, the 1619 assembly ruled that settlers who provided the Indians with "any shooting piece, shot, powder, or any other arms, offensive or defensive" would be hanged.

But the real hope for continued peace seemed to lie in the policy of Christianizing the Indians. In the first decade of the colony's existence no organized effort toward that end had been made (Pocahontas was the only notable convert of the early years). In the company's 1606 charter, conversion and education of the "sal-vages" had been envisioned. But it was not until 1619 that the company proceeded to raise money to build a school in Virginia that would train both white and Indian children according to Christian principles. With the enthusiastic backing of the king and the English clergy, sufficient funds were collected, and land was granted at a spot forty miles upriver from Jamestown.

The school site, later known as Dutch Gap, was in the Corporation of Henrico, the westernmost division of the colony—just short of the frontier foundry at Falling Creek. Sent

The Virginia settlers were encouraged to support themselves with a wide range of activities. An old English book pictured mining (far left), carpentry (left, above), farming (left, below), masonry (above), and bee-keeping (right, above). The first school (right, below), for Indian as well as white children, was authorized in 1619.

over to direct the establishment of the school was a prominent and devout English scholar, George Thorpe, recently a gentleman of the king's Privy Chamber. With him came fifty men to cultivate the school's lands and begin its construction.

Thorpe—this "most sufficient gentleman, virtuous and wise"—might conceivably have succeeded in his mission had it not already been too late. All opportunity for peaceful relations between the English and the Indians had undoubtedly ceased when Opechancanough took over the leadership of Powhatan's people in 1618.

He was a crafty and experienced leader, whose hostility to the white man is thought to have begun years before when he was defeated by the Spaniards in what is now the southwestern United States. Wandering in search of a new homeland for his followers, fighting his way through other tribes to the north and east, he came over the mountains to the region of Virginia's tidal rivers, the Tidewater. Powhatan had succeeded in making an alliance with the newly arrived chief, yet there was little harmony between them. Opechancanough recognized, where Powhatan did not, that there could be no compromise with the white men whose great winged ships forever brought new settlers. When Opechancanough assumed the leadership of the Powhatan Confederation, war was inevitable.

In the trustfulness of George Thorpe, Opechancanough saw he had a great weapon. Often and with increasing cordiality the chief came to Henrico to talk with the gentle scholar. Fearing nothing, Mr. Thorpe was delighted with Opechancanough's suggestion that an exchange of Indian and English youths be set up so that each could learn the other's ways. The assembly, and the company itself, also greeted the proposal as promising evidence that friendship might succeed where arms and armor had failed to make the wilderness secure; few reservations were expressed that the plan might lay the colony open to attack.

So friendly did the chief and Mr. Thorpe become that the latter had a house built for Opechancanough at Henrico "after the English fashion." So confident did the colony become of the chief's allegiance that he was allowed to pass through the colony and into Jamestown itself without question. And so successful was the exchange program that other Indians were invited to share the planters' lives, working with them in the fields, guiding them in the forests, and shooting game for their tables. No corner of the colony was unseen by curious Indian eyes. The law forbidding on pain of death the loan or sale of firearms to Indians had fallen silently into disuse. The time for the crippling attack that Opechancanough had long planned was now ripe.

If a spark was needed to set off the struggle, it was supplied when an Indian brave, Jack-of-the-Feathers, was asked by a planter named Morgan to guide him on a trading trip among the Indians. Jack soon returned, reporting that Morgan had been slain by hostile Indians, probably the Monacan. But when Morgan's servants saw that Jack had Morgan's cap, they insisted on taking him to Jamestown for questioning. The Indian refused. The white men shot and wounded him, put him in a boat, and started down the river for the capital. En route the captive died.

Chief Opechancanough admitted that he was "much grieved" by the incident, and it may have been then that the decision was made to put the plot into effect. His strategy had been carefully laid: by scouting each frontier community he had come to know how best to assign his braves at each strong point. They would attack simultaneously at eight o'clock on the morning of Good Friday, March 22, 1622; in one day of slaughter he hoped to wipe out the white man's inroads of many years.

The fateful morning dawned serenely. On most of the plantations that were marked for destruction the planters were already urging their families and workers out into the fields. Having breakfasted with their

In 1941 archaeologists at Jamestown un-earthed a large kiln comprising several hearths (above). In it the early colonists made much of their brick and tile. At top are two of the many iron building ornaments, including hinges and locks, also found at the Jamestown site. The glass bottles at left were put together from fragments discovered in the scientific excavations. Although some of the glass and ironware was made in Virginia, many items were imported from England.

107

white friends, the Indians now kept an eye cocked at the sun, watching for the angle of the eighth hour. In the woods beyond the cleared acres at Dutch Gap and Falling Creek, braves were waiting, cradling the weapons their white friends had given them, having reached their riverside posts in their white friends' boats.

At eight o'clock the Indians arose as one man, slaughtering, scalping, burning up and down the entire length of the James River valley. Bursting into the foundry, the Indians immedi-ately killed the mill master and his men and then fired the buildings and threw the machinery into the creek. It is not known with what early-morning devotions Mr. Thorpe had begun that Good Friday; but by a few minutes after eight his skull was split, and the houses at Henrico were in flames. Women and children, masters and servants, not a white person was spared as pillars of smoke rose one by one from the widely scattered settlements. Soon after the surprise attack had begun, some 350 colonists

Virginia Indians, before they possessed white men's firearms, used the long, powerful bows shown in this sixteenth-century engraving.

In Sidney King's painting Indians stealing through the forest on the day before the massacre of 1622 blend into the woodland growth.

lay dead (about a quarter of the colony's population), including John Rolfe and several other councilors.

The massacre would have produced more immediate victims if some colonists had not successfully fought back, wielding "spades, axes, and brickbats." Wherever a settler was able to get to his gun, the Indians fled, moving on to an easier target. Perhaps this was also a part of Opechancanough's plan. What happened in Jamestown was not.

The night before the massacre had been a sleepless one for an Indian boy named Chanco, who lived with the family of his white godfather, Richard Pace. Before the first light, the boy had made up his mind: he would not kill Pace as instructed. Instead, he woke him and told him of the plot. Hastily putting on his clothes, the settler leaped into his boat and rowed across the river to Jamestown to give the alarm. Muskets were quickly distributed from the arsenal, and the approaches were manned. After a few sallies by both land and water, the Indians withdrew.

Opechancanough's brilliant plot

In this version of the 1622 massacre, Indians plunder an outlying community as a war party in canoes

approaches Jamestown's fort (background).

had only half-succeeded, in part because of a Christianized Indian boy. The braves, with no plan for a follow-up attack, returned to their villages. But the end of the massacre of March 22 was by no means the end of death and destruction in the colony.

Governor Francis Wyatt, whose administration had begun at the end of Yeardley's three-year term, launched a series of reprisal campaigns against the Indians. Burning their villages, slaughtering their families, destroying their crops, the governor's men by indiscriminate ravages succeeded in alienating all the Indian tribes in the Tidewater, even those who had not been allied with Opechancanough.

The reduced colony's plight was made more desperate by disease. As the colonists abandoned the farther-out settlements and drew back to live together in the closely packed houses of Jamestown, a terrible plague was given new fuel. It raged unchecked through family after family, with the result that twice as many colonists were lost as in the massacre itself.

As great as was the loss of life and the loss of property in the massacre and in the successive plagues of 1622 and 1623, the loss of hope was even greater. The generous expectations of the burgesses and the councilors of 1619—that the colony could prosper on the basis of an intelligent plan drafted in London with opportunity and tolerance for all—were dreams that now seemed to stand little chance of being realized.

6

MUTINY AND

The Latin motto on the colony's coat of arms means "Virginia made up the fifth part." Britain's other parts were England, Scotland, Ireland, and Wales.

REBELLION

COLONIAL WILLIAMSBURG

In the summer of 1623 the report came to London that settlers were dying in the streets of Jamestown. Grim indeed had been the preceding winter, grimmer still the summer. Hunger and disease seemed to be the twin scourges of the colony. None of the steps the London Company took —such as seeing to it that immigrants arrived only in the fall, after the summer season of high mortality had passed—were wise enough or bold enough, apparently, to take the colony out of its difficulties.

The English investors, apprised of these reports, grumbled with increasing discontent. Many of them still hoped that their venture in the New World would give them quick profits —such as the rich cargoes of silk and spices that sailed into the wharves of the East India Company or the gleaming produce of Spain's overseas gold and silver mines. But all Virginia seemed to produce, besides tobacco, was a need for more and more money. If it had not been for public lotteries and subscriptions, people said, the company and its colony would have failed years before.

These malicious rumors, fed by consistently exaggerated reports of the desperate condition of the colonists, eventually reached the king's ears—just as they had been intended to do. For many of these reports had been inspired by men who thought they saw a possible advantage to themselves in bringing about the ruin of the London Company. They hoped that a monopoly might be formed through which they could control all production and sale of tobacco and thus grow fat on Virginia's troublesome weed.

The king himself was not reluctant to contemplate the company's downfall, particularly when he learned that the colonists were about to receive an even more liberal charter, drafted by Sandys in 1621. Whether in England or overseas, the virtue of a popular government was beyond the range of James' narrow vision; to him the company's establishment of the House of Burgesses was a mistake that badly needed rectifying.

When the colonists began to get wind of the ill-favor that the company was falling into, they at once sprang to the defense of Sandys and his fellow directors. Their protests had the effect of dispatching an investigating commission to Virginia. Unfortunately, the commission's report seemed to confirm the worst of the rumors: it called the colony, with its representative government and independent spirit, "a seminary of sedition."

But fight as the colonists might, the company's days were numbered. The king brought legal action against the company to get its directors to accept a new and totally undemocratic charter that he had prepared. Sandys and his colleagues finally appealed to Parliament, petitioning that body to join them in rejecting the king's demands. James, knowing that the English Parliament was too unsure of itself to dance any tune but his, instructed its leaders to ignore the petition. They obeyed, with only "soft mutterings." Then, on May 24, 1624, the Court of The King's Bench revoked the company's charter on a small technicality. Thus the London Company, which for seventeen years had been trying to keep Virginia alive as an intelligent experiment in New World development, found itself dissolved.

After some months of censorship, the news eventually reached Jamestown that the king had disbanded the company and that henceforth Virginia would be ruled as a royal colony by the king himself and his appointees. The news was received with dismay; there was understandable concern that the colony's freedoms and privileges were lost forever. But one of the commissioners who had been sent to Jamestown to investigate the true condition of the colony, a short-tempered military man, Captain John Harvey, failed to make note of the colonists' anxiety when he returned to England early in 1625. On the basis of his limited judgments and their own desires, the king's appointees then decided not to recommend re-establishing the colony's General Assembly. It appeared that the worst fears of the colonists were to be justified.

In a more generous move, the king's advisers recommended that Governor Wyatt be kept at his post, though that popular gentleman had

England's new king, the shy but obstinate Charles I (1625–49), is shown in the upper left-hand panel above. His execution, which scandalized Virginians, is re-enacted in the four other scenes.

married a niece of Sandys' and had by no means disapproved of the London Company's liberal policies. If they thought they could make Wyatt into the very model of an unquestioning colonial governor, James' advisers were wrong: one of the governor's first acts upon learning of the royal takeover was to call a special convention of Virginia's planters. The purpose of this emergency meeting was to address a petition to the king demanding the preservation of the colonists' liberties and, more particularly, the preservation of the General Assembly.

More than a decade passed, however, before the colonists' petition was answered—favorably—by King Charles I, James' son. It was a period during which the colony did not succumb to all of the perils that the commissioners had spotted after the massacre. Rather, it was a time of enormous growth and vitality in Virginia. There was a building boom in Jamestown itself, with finished wooden and brick buildings constructed that were a far cry from the humble daub and wattle structures of the past. In 1630 the council decided to build row houses in the capital, with a whole block of structures sharing common

walls, just as they did in London. In 1634 the first grammar school in the colony was built at Hampton across the James River in Elizabeth City County.

Not only in Jamestown but all along the James the colony grew. And it grew even more expansively under the aggressive leadership of Sir John Harvey—the same John Harvey who had been an unpopular commissioner in the early twenties—knighted now but no pleasanter. Governor Harvey made a special land offer to settlers who would "plant" on the York River. His theory was that the best way to defend the colony against Opechancanough's Indians was not by withdrawal but by settlement in force throughout the high-ridged strip of land running between the James and the York rivers. The final part of Harvey's plan for expansion was to run a four-mile palisade of high, spiked pilings over the ridge between the two rivers—or actually between tributaries of the rivers. The palisade would keep the Indians out of the settled area and keep livestock in.

Responding to Harvey's leadership, the colony once again began to flex its muscles and assert itself. One of the ways in which the colony expressed its new energy and confidence was by getting rid of Harvey.

He had always been a short-tempered individual. And despite his farsighted measures, his contempt for the colonists' rights and traditions was no secret. Soon after he arrived as governor in 1630, he had the acting governor—a hard-drinking, well-liked physician, Dr. John Pott—arrested. Dr. Pott had been the first settler at the head of Archer's Hope Creek, site of a community known first as Middle Plantation and later as Williamsburg. After an all too hasty trial by hand-picked jurors, the doctor was convicted on two counts, one of which was the rather common offense of marking other men's cattle as his own. Only because of the loyalty of his wife (who took ship to London and successfully presented an appeal to the king) and because of intervention by Harvey himself (who feared losing one of the colony's few medical men) was Dr. Pott saved from the loss of all

ST. LUKE'S RESTORATION

The ivy-covered tower of the Jamestown church (left) is thought to have been constructed in 1639. The rest of the church was rebuilt along the lines of the equally old St. Luke's Church, Smithfield (above).

he possessed. Then there was the incident in which Governor Harvey knocked out the teeth of a councilor with his cudgel during an altercation in the council chamber. These stormy events helped persuade the planters that their governor had to go.

Even more painful reasons for the widespread sentiment against Governor Harvey lay in his apparent willingness to help the king's friends achieve their long-desired purpose of establishing a tobacco monopoly. Also, for personal motives (perhaps merely to curry favor), Harvey seemed cordially disposed toward the Catholic settlers who in 1634 occupied a king's grant in Maryland that the militantly Protestant Virginians considered theirs.

In April, 1635, therefore, a special assembly was convened to consider the colonists' grievances against the governor. Ignoring Harvey's order to

disband, and amid cries of treason on both sides, the councilors persuaded Sir John to return to England for judgment. Harvey was acquitted the following year, for in the time of England's Stuart kings it was unthinkable to have a royal representative "thrust out." But by 1639, after the mutinous sentiments had cooled somewhat, Sir John Harvey was permanently removed from office. To anyone who could see, it was clear that these Vir-

The palisade built over the ridge between the James and York rivers terminated at about this point—a broad bay on King Creek, which is a tributary of the York. Sites such as this were claimed by bold Virginia planters in the expansive times after 1624.

ginians, whose rights seemed at one point to be vanishing, were willing to fight to preserve them.

At last the news came that King Charles had granted the colonists' petition of 1625; the "liberty of general assembly" would be guaranteed. These glad tidings were brought from England by Sir Francis Wyatt, who had agreed to serve one more term as governor of Virginia (1639–42) before retiring from his long life of service to the colony.

During Wyatt's administration, and during the first term of his successor, Sir William Berkeley, a number of reforms were enacted that contributed to the hope that the royal representatives were becoming more understanding of the Virginians' needs and desires. Regular meetings of the General Assembly were held, and the two houses began to meet separately —which had the effect of encouraging the burgesses to speak out more freely. In addition, the method of selecting the burgesses was modified to keep up with the growth of the colony's new counties. Along with stricter laws to regulate the quality of Virginia tobacco came the introduction of coins in the place of tobacco receipts, which made trading considerably easier. For the first time taxation was revised to account for the size of a planter's holdings and his ability to pay.

Sir William Berkeley posed for the portrait above during his second term as governor (1660–76). His wife, also portrayed above, was considered to be one of the colony's most beautiful women.

In this painting by the illustrator Howard Pyle, Governor Berkeley (seated) receives a commissioner sent from England to set up a Virginia government more to Parliament's liking.

Perhaps the most popular of Sir William Berkeley's reforms was his repeal of the poll tax, which, under previous administrations, each colonist had had to pay to the governor. This action, which favored the smaller planters, seemed characteristic of the young and energetic Sir William, who had come to Virginia at the age of thirty-four, leaving behind in London a successful social and literary life. While charming the leading planters with his grace and intelligence, he won further favor with the less affluent colonists by negotiating peace with Virginia's colonial neighbors in the Chesapeake Bay area and by initiating a series of expeditions to explore land to the west. New land beyond the mountains, gold mines, a glimpse of the fabled South Sea—all of these possibilities dazzled the poor farmers, many of whom had but a few worked-out acres to cultivate.

121

On Governor Berkeley's plantation, Green Spring, he conducted agricultural experiments and led a gentlemanly life. In the late 1700's, the American architect Benjamin Latrobe painted this view of Green Spring, by then much enlarged.

Two great events then interrupted Sir William's remarkable career. The first was the devastating massacre of 1644, Opechancanough's final attempt to obliterate the white man's settlements. Berkeley quickly rallied the colonists and waged a vigorous war against the Indians. So successful was his campaign that the Indians at last sued for peace, and a treaty was drawn up in 1646. Not for three decades would the Virginia Indians be a serious threat to the Tidewater plantations.

The second event that threatened to halt Sir William's progress was the struggle between the king and the Parliament that had broken out in 1640, which came to be called the Great Rebellion. At its end the Parliamentary forces of the Puritan leader Oliver Cromwell defeated King Charles, and the execution of the king followed in 1649. During these years of uncertainty, during which many of the king's men (called Cavaliers) fled to Virginia, Berkeley tried to keep the Virginians neutral, though he himself was fiercely royalist in his outlook.

When finally a strong English fleet

These three Indians, tribesmen of the Powhatan Confederation, were painted by a Swiss artist in 1701.

123

bearing new men to replace Berkeley's royalist councilors appeared at the mouth of the James, the governor marshaled an armed force to resist it. But ultimately, after seeing to it that his threat of bloodshed produced the most favorable terms, the governor agreed to retire to his plantation.

Under the Commonwealth, as Oliver Cromwell's regime was called, Virginia enjoyed a startling upsurge— a period of economic and democratic growth that was never forgotten. In keeping with reforms in England, there were neither trade restrictions nor taxes in Virginia. The House of Burgesses, which had heretofore been regarded as the least powerful sector of colonial government, now found itself given the responsibility of electing both the councilors and the governor himself.

But when the news came to Virginia that Cromwell had died (1658) and that the Stuart kings would surely be restored, the burgesses began to pay court to their royalist and still popular former governor. Sir William Berkeley, visited by a delegation of burgesses at his sprawling plantation, Green Spring, was asked if he would serve again as governor, on condition that he vow allegiance to whatever government would emerge from the chaos of English politics. Ever the royalist, Berkeley declared his alle-

Governor Berkeley tries in vain to enlist Gloucester County men against Bacon.

giance to the Stuarts only, and this the assembly delegates had to accept.

From this moment on, and after his re-appointment by the king, Sir William's self-importance increased enormously—and his popularity declined.

The first group to be antagonized by Berkeley during his second term of office (1660–76) were the small planters and the frontiersmen. The governor re-instituted many of the taxes that had formerly plagued the Virginians and formed a government that ignored the colony's more democratic elements. The Cavaliers and the newly rich aristocrats who flocked about him paid little heed to the cries of injustice that were raised against the clique of large planters and English merchants. And on the fringe of the Tidewater plantations, settlers found that their interests were second to those of unscrupulous traders who wished to preserve good relations with the Indians under any circumstances.

At this moment there rose to prominence in the colony a man who, like a few others in history, was superbly gifted to take advantage of popular discontent—and to turn it into something greater.

His name was Nathaniel Bacon. The only son of an English country squire and a cousin of the great chancellor Francis Bacon, he had been educated at Cambridge University

The illustrations on these pages are from old histories of the United States. Pictured below is one of the early events of Bacon's Rebellion: Bacon's men attempt to force an Indian village by fording a stream. Later, Bacon defeated the warring Indians.

and had gone on to prove himself a brilliant law student. Then, having toured Europe and married an aristocratic lady, against her father's will, he had set out to Virginia to improve his fortune. Twenty-seven when he arrived there in 1674, he settled at Curle's Neck, forty miles above Jamestown, and started to work.

As a gentleman of good education and breeding, whose cousin was a much-respected councilor, the young newcomer was soon admitted to the council. There he began to notice Governor Berkeley's lordly ways, which were so offensive to his fellow Virginians.

For sixteen years after his re-installation, Berkeley refused to allow a new House of Burgesses to be elected. Content to be surrounded by old conservative friends, he showered them with large gifts and tax favors. Though this may have been standard procedure in the courts of seventeenth-century Europe, it was viewed with bitterness by Bacon and other independent-minded farmers of Virginia. They were also disposed to put the blame on Berkeley for a procession of calamities that then visited the colony —bad crops, sickness of men and animals alike, and ever new taxes imposed by the king.

It also seemed to Bacon that Sir William's policy of laxity toward the Indians was motivated more by Berkeley's beaver-trading interests than by wisdom. And when a band of Doeg and Susquehannock Indians

From the steps of the court house at Middle Plantation, Bacon reads a proclamation to his rebellious followers. The historic event has been recreated by a modern artist.

took to the warpath, one of the plantations they attacked was Bacon's. His overseer was brutally murdered. Believing that he could expect no real help from the colonial government, and knowing that he would not be able to get a commission to proceed against the Indians, Bacon decided on a rash course of action.

Meeting with a group of irate Charles City planters in 1676, Nathaniel Bacon promised revenge. "If the Redskins meddle with me, I will harry them, commission or no commission," he shouted. These and other such ringing sentiments convinced many oppressed farmers and workers that this was the leader who might bring back the better conditions they had enjoyed under the Commonwealth. Bacon had, apparently, no real intention of starting a crusade—merely an Indian expedition—but his rabble-rousing words now put him at the head of a zealous mob.

If he lacked moderation and patience, at least he was not short on courage or intelligence. Though the Indian policy was the most pressing problem that Bacon sought to correct, questions of fair play and freedom were also at stake. He began to formulate ideas about taxes, voting, elections, and privileges that perhaps one day he hoped to see made into the law of the land. "Finding that the country was basely, for a small, sordid gain, betrayed, and the lives of the poor inhabitants wretchedly sacrificed," the rebellious Bacon wrote to an English friend, "I resolved to stand in this ruinous gap, risking my life and fortune to all hazards."

The hot-headed young man asked the governor for a commission to lead his volunteers against the Indians. But Berkeley, recognizing that Bacon's men had more passion than judgment, feared that by indiscriminate slaughter they would stir up the western frontier and shatter the network of native treaties he was trying to maintain. When no reply came from Jamestown, Bacon and seventy men marched anyway.

Slaughter it was indeed; Bacon's men gave no quarter among the Indian villages. Hearing this, Berkeley declared them rebels. But when he saw that the colony strongly supported Bacon, the governor backed down. For the first time in ten years he called for the election of a new House of Burgesses and for a meeting of the General Assembly to air complaints. Bacon, though captured by the governor's soldiers, was pardoned and re-instated in the council. It was clear that the younger man had won the first round.

But the fight was far from over. Troublemakers on both sides kept old flames alive. Advised that there was a murder plot against him, Bacon left Jamestown under cover of darkness. Rallying his men, he returned with six hundred followers on June 23, 1676. They marched to the State House where Berkeley and the House of Burgesses were meeting. Brave if not always prudent, Berkeley came out, denounced Bacon, and tore open his own shirt.

"Here! Shoot me—'fore God, fair mark. Shoot!" he cried.

When the rebels did not shoot, Berkeley drew his sword and challenged Bacon to a personal duel.

"Sir," Bacon replied politely, "I came not, nor intend, to hurt a hair on your Honor's head. And as for your sword, your Honor may please to put

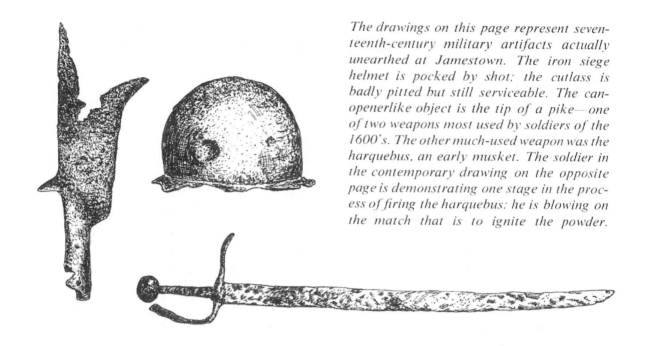

The drawings on this page represent seventeenth-century military artifacts actually unearthed at Jamestown. The iron siege helmet is pocked by shot; the cutlass is badly pitted but still serviceable. The can-openerlike object is the tip of a pike—one of two weapons most used by soldiers of the 1600's. The other much-used weapon was the harquebus, an early musket. The soldier in the contemporary drawing on the opposite page is demonstrating one stage in the process of firing the harquebus: he is blowing on the match that is to ignite the powder.

it up; it shall rust in its scabbard before ever I shall desire you to draw it. I come for a commission against the heathen who daily inhumanly murder us and spill our brethrens blood. And a commission I will have before I go!"

Then Bacon gave an order to his men: "Prime your guns!" Seeing that he meant what he said, the frightened burgesses quickly gave in. Commissions for Bacon and thirty of his men were drawn up and signed by Berkeley. Moreover, five acts known as Bacon's Laws were hastily approved: a thousand men under Bacon were allowed to march against the Indians; members of the council were required to pay taxes like everyone else; a freeman was allowed to vote whether or not he owned property; the people were allowed to elect members of the county

court; and the number of persons holding office and drawing money from the colonial government was to be reduced.

On June 26 the triumphant Bacon set out to fight the Indians. Once he had gone, Berkeley tried to get the regular militia to pursue him. Rather than discouraging Bacon, such opposition only persuaded him, and his followers, that they were embarked upon a cause that could only triumph with the defeat of the governor in battle.

Having issued a wordy Declaration to the People, which indicted Berkeley and his administration, Bacon then tried to rally wide support. On August 3 he called a meeting at Middle Plantation, asking "prime gentlemen" to help him bring about

GHEYN, *Maniement d'Armes*, 1608

peace and reorganize the government. Sixty-nine came and signed a declaration that the authority of Berkeley was over. Copies of this were sent to justices of the peace, with orders to have citizens swear to accept it. Many did, out of enthusiasm, or fear, or both, and Berkeley, realizing that his support was in the minority, fled across the Chesapeake to the Eastern Shore.

Bacon immediately made plans to pursue Berkeley by water, and he was able to seize and arm two vessels in the James for that purpose. Another vessel, unfortunately for the young rebel, escaped his grasp and set sail for England, bearing the news of Berkeley's flight to the king. In command of the larger of Bacon's two commandeered ships were his lieu-

tenants William Carver and Miles Bland. They carelessly left a captain and crew aboard who were friendly to Berkeley, and the ship on which so much had depended ended up in Berkeley's hands. For their blunder both Carver and Bland were executed by Bacon.

Boarding the captured ship, Governor Berkeley returned to Jamestown on September 8. No one opposed his landing, so he was free to begin rallying forces for an all-out battle. Bacon was ready for a final test too. Five days later he drew up his little army in the "Green Spring Old Field," just above Jamestown, and posted lookouts. A pitched battle followed.

For a while it looked as if the royalist forces under Berkeley would hold; then they turned and ran, leaving Bacon the victory. The rebels, bent on vengeance, decided to put Jamestown to the torch. And in their passion to remove all traces of the old regime and to insure that Berkeley would find nothing of value if he returned, they even set their own homes ablaze. It is estimated that total losses reached a value of 1,500,000 pounds of tobacco.

Moving on to Green Spring, Berkeley's mansion, Bacon drew up a loyalty oath for Virginians to take. If the English government tried to suppress the people's rights, he said, those troops must be resisted; and if the pressure became too great, the settlers could leave the Tidewater and make homes for themselves in the western

129

CITIZENS
OF JAMESTOWN

The handsome ruin at right was once the Jamestown home of the clever-looking gentleman in the portrait below—Edward Jaquelin, second husband of the widow of Virginia's attorney general at the time of Bacon's Rebellion. Jaquelin built the roomy brick structure about 1710, when the decline of Jamestown, which had begun after the rebellion, was well advanced. Another property holder who refused to forsake the old port-city was William Brodnax, whose portrait appears on the opposite page. Pictured beside their respective fathers are Elizabeth Jaquelin (holding a rose) and Elizabeth Brodnax (with laurel leaves). The portraits were painted in 1722 by an anonymous American artist who posed his subjects in the approved English style but still managed to capture the charm and individuality of these four citizens of decaying Jamestown.

part of Virginia. Pardoning his prisoners and passing strict laws against looting and stealing, Bacon tried to reknit the shattered fabric of government. Whatever his faults, he seemed anxious to bring a greater measure of democracy to the colony.

That objective was all too obvious to the Crown when news of the rebellion reached London. Plainly, King Charles would have to take action. On October 3 he appointed Herbert Jeffreys, Sir John Berry, and Colonel Francis Moryson to sail immediately to investigate matters in Virginia.

But it was death, not the king, that intervened in Bacon's plans. Overtaxed by months of strain and exposure, the young leader died in Gloucester County, across the York River, of "lice and flux," on October 26, 1676. To prevent mutilation of his body by vengeful royalists, his followers buried him secretly in a remote inlet. To this day the exact burial place is not known.

When word came of Bacon's death, the defeated Berkeley sprang into action. Returning from the Eastern Shore, where he had fled after the September battle, he found no lack of Virginians ready to rally to his aristocratic cause. Without their leader, the rebels were driven from the field; one after another they were captured, court-martialed, and executed. Having routed the disorganized rebels, Berkeley indulged in an orgy of revenge.

In January of 1677, the commissioners sent to investigate the rebellion arrived from England. The one thousand troops accompanying them camped at Jamestown, where the destruction wrought by the rebel army was so widespread that the commissioners themselves stayed across the river in Thomas Swann's home. Whether or not Jamestown would be restored was for a while in doubt. The House of Burgesses passed a resolution suggesting that the capital be moved to Tindall's Point in Gloucester County across the York River, but this was not acceptable to the Crown. Later, royal instructions provided for the rebuilding of Jamestown.

Meanwhile, friction between Berkeley and the commissioners mounted. In February, 1677, Jeffreys presented his commission as lieutenant governor, plus the papers providing for Berkeley's recall. When Berkeley refused to relinquish his authority, Jeffreys finally declared himself to be governor, to Berkeley's dismay. At last, the embittered old man sailed for England on May 5. He arrived there too sick to appear at court. Only fifteen months after Bacon's Rebellion began, Sir William Berkeley died, disillusioned and discouraged. The career that began so brilliantly ended tragically.

Bacon's Rebellion was in itself a disastrous event; yet it served an important purpose in proving to all the world that Virginians would not only rise in anger against arbitrary rule but would die struggling for the rights that they thought were theirs.

With the end of the Bacon Rebellion came an end to the wars with the coastal Indians. This silver medal was presented to the Potomac Indians upon the signing of the treaty of 1677.

7

The rebellion was over, and Sir William Berkeley was in his grave. But most of Virginia's vexing problems remained alive. The beneficial laws that Nathaniel Bacon had pushed through the assembly were repealed in 1677; money was scarce, as was the opportunity for the poorer workers to get ahead; overproduction of tobacco was forcing prices down and tempers up.

The new governor who sailed into the ruined and garrisoned capital city of Jamestown in 1680, Lord Culpeper, was not greatly concerned with the difficulties of the tobacco industry. To him what mattered most was his own enrichment, which he had assumed would come naturally as a result of his appointment as a royal governor. When he took a year's trip to England in 1681 on a matter of personal business, he commanded the assembly not to meet until his return. This had the unfortunate effect of preventing the Virginia legislators from passing any laws that might control tobacco production. The burgesses had hoped to stop the planting and harvesting of one entire year's growth, believing that scarcity might finally give a boost to the lagging price of their only product. In the absence of such wise legislation, hotter heads began to make up their own solutions. After first destroying the young tobacco plants in their own fields and in those of their neighbors, bands of planters roamed the countryside, often by night, "cutting out" the crops of other settlers. This brutal and illegal means of con-

THE VIRGINIANS

COLLEGE OF WILLIAM AND MARY; COURTESY COLONIAL WILLIAMSBURG

Though Jamestown eventually recovered from Bacon's Rebellion, the capital was moved in 1699 to Middle Plantation (Williamsburg), site of William and Mary College (background).

trolling the colony's tobacco production could not of course be tolerated, and repressive measures were taken as soon as Governor Culpeper returned.

Fortunately, a rise in tobacco prices occurred at nearly the same time (1683), and the tense colony relaxed somewhat, enjoying one of its first peaceful years since Bacon's Rebellion. So relaxed was the mood of the colony (and so clear was it to the governor that he would never make a fortune in Virginia) that Lord Culpeper decided to sail off to his home in England, without the king's permission—where he paid for his willfulness with his job. Then, after a brief term by Lieutenant Governor Nicholas Spencer, the reins of colonial government were assumed by Lord Howard in 1684.

Not even Governor Berkeley had been a more dedicated enemy of the colonists' long tradition of independence than was Lord Howard. This overbearing representative of England's Charles II made it as clear as possible to the Virginians that their assembly was by no means an overseas version of the English Parliament, that the king could counter any one of their actions, and that Lord Howard himself was capable of undermining their most sacred institutions.

To intimidate the House of Burgesses, Howard dismissed its clerk and appointed his own man to that important office. In the critical decade following Bacon's Rebellion, the burgesses were stripped of three major

powers: their right to decide how to spend tax revenues, their right to hear judicial appeals, and their right to elect their own clerk. However, they successfully defended their fundamental right to levy taxes.

Thus they learned, by intense political activity, how to live with England's heavy-handed rule—by frustrating it, not by venturing into the mutiny and rebellion of the preceding generation. And in the process of defending the colony's representative government, these aristocratically inclined leaders won the respect and support of all classes of Virginians.

Yet in the political deadlock between the Crown and the colonists, neither side could really win. Nor could the colony improve its lot until it found a way to break out of its economic and geographic limitations.

By the 1680's the colonists had settled most of the territory of the Tidewater. In this great fertile basin the early history of the colony had been enacted. Originally the land was rich and open to all, but by the final quarter of the seventeenth century, its soil had become worked out by tobacco, and its society had become increasingly restrictive. What was needed was a revolutionary event that would liberate the energies and the minds of the Virginians.

When it came, it occurred not in Virginia but in England. It was called the Glorious Revolution. Engineered by Parliament, it was a popular and bloodless uprising against the last of

England's Glorious Revolution (1688) brought the Protestant monarchs William and Mary to the throne, a welcome development for Virginians who had distrusted their Catholic predecessor, James II.

the Stuart kings, James II, who had succeeded to the throne upon the death of his brother in 1685. Bull-headed and totally unaware of the changing nature of the times, he affirmed the position taken by his grandfather, James I: an English king could make and unmake laws by his own will. As a final indignity to Protestant England, James II's infant son, born in 1688, was baptized a Roman Catholic. This act opened up the intolerable prospect of an indefinite line of Catholic rulers. The nation's leaders revolted resolutely and triumphantly.

Word of the Glorious Revolution came to Virginia in April of 1689,

after months of rumors. Finally, it was ascertained that as a result of Parliament's swift and effective action, James II had fled into exile, his Protestant daughter Mary and her ambitious husband, William of Orange, had been invited to cross over from Holland to reign, and the pair had been declared corulers of England and Scotland. Glorious indeed did the revolution sound to the colonists, who saw at once that just as Parliament had triumphed over the Stuarts, so would the Virginia assembly now be strengthened in its disputes with royal representatives. Jamestown rang with the discharge of muskets, the beating

137

The removal of the colonial capital to Williamsburg marked the beginning of Jamestown's decline, and by the time of the Revolution the town had been abandoned. During the Civil War, a Confederate fort was built on the site, but when this water color was painted in 1865, little other than an old church tower and a weed-choked cemetery remained.

138

of drums, and the joyous shouts of free men.

In other English colonies the momentous news produced uprisings against officials who had been appointed by the former king. But fortunately for the safety of his hide, Lord Howard had left Virginia in December, 1688, and had arrived in London the following February. Even there he could not escape the contentious colonists. The actions of his administration and the complaints of the Virginians were reviewed on order of King William by the Privy Council's Committee on Trade and Plantations. The solution was a masterful compromise, in keeping with the fresh spirit of reasonableness that had entered England with the new monarchs. Lord Howard was to keep the post of governor, as evidence that his actions had not been improper, but he would remain in England, while a newly appointed lieutenant governor—Captain Francis Nicholson, who had a reputation for sympathetic understanding of the colonists—would go to Virginia to take on the actual administration.

Virginia at last seemed rid of the crippling political quarrels that had marked her past and was ready to enter upon an age of relative harmony and growth. Many other problems remained, to be sure; among them her closed society (plus the closed minds that went with it) and the dangers of her one-crop economy. But these difficulties too could be eased, given leaders who knew the country and its increasingly distinct breed of people.

By a curious coincidence, on the very day that the General Assembly witnessed the swearing in of its trim and soldierly lieutenant governor (June 3, 1690), the councilors and burgesses also heard a clerk read the official commission of a newly appointed representative of the Bishop of London. This zealous young Scottish minister, named James Blair and called Commissary Blair in recognition of his special appointment, had already served in the colony for five years as superintendent of church affairs and had been uniquely successful in that capacity. Though sharptongued and tactless, he respected the Virginians' way of life, and he was to prove just as effective in his own sphere as Lieutenant Governor Nicholson was in his.

While Nicholson moved vigorously ahead to reorganize the militia, court the local belles, and improve economic conditions, Blair looked into the minds and hearts of his fellow Christians and concluded that growth would be limited unless more and better education was made available. While Nicholson instituted annual foot races, wrestling matches, and other athletic contests, which were jokingly called "Olympick Games," Blair recommended to the General Assembly that a free school and college be established that would be known as the College of William and Mary in Virginia. The friendly, matching endeavors of Blair and Nicholson

at first seemed to be the best sort of competition; it was only later that the two young leaders became bitter rivals.

For the moment, Nicholson, who was no less interested in the arts than in athletics, gave the college project his hearty support. And, having been empowered by the assembly to carry a petition for support to London, Blair arrived at court and knelt before the king on November 12, 1691. Because of the commissary's efforts, a charter was eventually issued. A Crown grant of about two thousand pounds and the income from twenty thousand acres of land was made, and Blair (the General Assembly's nomi-

A sketch of 1702 by a visitor to William and Mary College is the only known view of the school's first building, burned in 1705.

nee) was appointed the college's first president. When he made a report of his successful mission to the assembly in Jamestown in October, 1693, the burgesses and councilors expressed their thanks to King William and Queen Mary. Then they made a fateful decision: they resolved that the college should be built not in the capital, but at Middle Plantation. Despite memories that that flourishing little community (patented by Dr. John Pott in 1632) had served as a storm center for Bacon's Rebellion, the decision was both popular and logical.

It was a broad, elevated site, only seven miles from the capital by land but far removed in terms of what might be expected of it. Low-lying Jamestown was a cramped warren of little medieval houses and malodorous alleyways swept by fires and disease; Middle Plantation by contrast seemed healthful and open, offering room enough for indefinite expansion. Traveling up to the frontier settlement, Blair and his teaching colleagues (Mungo Ingles, a "writing master," and an usher named Mulliken) soon found quarters for themselves and for the boys who became the college's first students. By 1695 the foundations were put in for the college's own building, which would stand at one end of a horse path (later a broad street—see page 135) that led along the main ridge and past the church. The building was an unusually handsome brick structure that was probably designed by the great English architect Sir Christopher Wren.

The good judgment of the assembly in not locating the college in Jamestown seemed to be further confirmed when in 1698 (the year of the Wren building's completion) the recently completed State House in the capital burned to the ground—the fourth state house to be destroyed by fire. When committee members of the assembly journeyed up to Middle Plantation the following spring to consider whether the capital might be moved there, or to any other possible site, they found that the construction of the college had started a small boom. As well as the church, there were two mills, several stores, an inn, and a smith's shop—all positioned according to the natural contours of the land.

The May Day celebrations of 1699 in the little college town were generally viewed as a significant milestone in the colony's history. The students chosen to speak tried to match the occasion with their rhetoric. "Methinks," one said, "we see already that happy time when we shall surpass the [Asiatic] in civility, the Egyptians in geometry, the Phoenicians in arithmetic, and the Chaldeans in astrology. O happy Virginia!"

Impressed by such youthful eloquence, the legislators formally resolved to make Middle Plantation the capital; its name would be changed to Williamsburg in honor of the king whose accession had already produced so many blessings for the colony.

"O happy Virginia" seemed not

In the last quarter of the seventeenth century, the aristocratic planters of Virginia began to build handsome mansions on the James. Westover, thirty miles upriver from Jamestown, was begun by William Byrd in 1690; his son, William Byrd II, later rebuilt it in brick. A neighbor's daughter, Lucy Harrison, painted Westover in 1825 (below).

too wild a compliment to pay to the colony—with its ambitious college and its plans for a new capital. A generation of Virginians was then being born and would grow up in an atmosphere that for the first time could be called both civilized and American.

This fortunate new period of Virginia's history was by no means a time of opportunity for the com-

mon man. Opportunity for the small farmer was a thing of the past, and emigration to other colonies was the only choice for thousands of Virginia families who found they could no longer survive in the land of large, slave-worked plantations. But this was a period of greatness, nonetheless —of great opportunity for the few. It saw the establishment of many of America's leading families, the beginning of American literature in the South, and the dream of westward adventure.

All of those themes were gathered together in the life of one colorful Virginian of this period, William Byrd II, who returned to his native Virginia from schooling in England upon his father's death in 1704. The

elder Byrd had once allied himself with Nathaniel Bacon but had broken away when it appeared that that firebrand was interested in economic reforms as well as in Indian fighting. By the end of his life, the senior William Byrd was president of the council and one of the colony's most successful planters and traders. His son, a handsome young man with deep-set eyes and a large nose, had already been elected to the House of Burgesses and had scored other personal successes in the colony while still in his twenties. But now there was a ques-

The first capitol at Williamsburg, an H-shaped structure with separate wings for the General Court and the House of Burgesses, was built in 1701–5 and razed by fire in 1747. The 1931–34 reconstruction below was based on the 1730 engraving above.

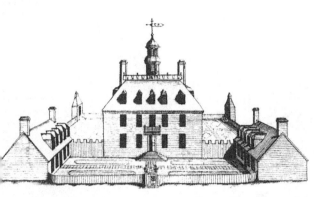

Williamsburg's social life centered on the stately Governor's Palace, built in 1706–20 and burned to the ground in 1781. The reconstruction below follows the plan of the eighteenth-century engraving above, with the kitchens and stables in two side buildings.

tion whether this elegant young man had the courage and tenacity to step into his father's shoes. What good would his love of the classics, his fondness for English society, and his interest in architecture and science do him on his father's vast lands in this raw young country?

Young Byrd immediately moved into the large house his father had recently built about thirty miles from Jamestown, called Westover, and proceeded to put one of his talents to good use: he found himself a suitable bride, Lucy Parke, whom he married

Once the early hardships of settlement had been overcome, Virginia adopted the gracious way of life for which it is still famous. An unknown primitive artist painted this scene of Virginians fox hunting.

in 1706. A spitfire of a girl, she unfortunately brought her husband more headaches (plus her family's debts) than he had bargained for, but her social connections were impeccable. By 1709, Byrd had a growing family himself—the permanence of the Byrd dynasty seemed to be assured—and he found himself named to the council.

He doubtless hoped to settle down to the aristocratic pleasures of helping run the church and the government, writing his diary, overseeing his estates, and rebuilding Westover according to more fashionable architec-

tural patterns. In all of these he made a beginning. Gradually he was able to transform his father's wooden house into a Georgian mansion (pages 142–143). It was a masterpiece of symmetry, noble in proportions and balance. One of Westover's most impressive features was the library, generally held to be the best in the colonies. Started by Byrd's father, it eventually contained more than 3,600 volumes on philosophy, history, law, travel, literature—in Greek, Latin, Hebrew, and more modern languages—the passport to all lands and ages. Into

146

one or another of these volumes, Byrd dipped each day; and with equal conscientiousness, he prayed, exercised, and observed the passing of the seasons.

But neither his own temperament, nor his finances (which were undermined by his wife's family's debts), nor the needs of Virginia allowed him to fit into a life of passive enjoyment. The increasingly powerful Commissary Blair had at length succeeded in besting his rival, Francis Nicholson. Nicholson, who had been appointed governor in 1698, had tangled with both Blair (in the matter of administering the college) and the council (in the matter of taxes) and had finally been removed from Virginia in 1705.

Now another controversy arose, with Blair and the councilors on one side and the new lieutenant governor, Alexander Spotswood, on the other. Lieutenant Governor Spotswood had had the audacity to suggest that courts might be established that would not be responsible to the council and would hear some of the complaints of the small farmers. For this suggestion he was almost removed from office by the Blair faction. However, William Byrd II, asked to explain the matter to the Board of Trade in London, was eventually able to cool the tempers of all parties. Here he began to show that education and a measure of charm were great assets in the New World. The role that Byrd would play for the rest of his life—which has been called that of "the Great American Gentle-man"—began to be recognized as useful to the Virginia of his day.

Though Byrd may have been reluctant to leave his gracious home to take on this role of public leadership, doing so mostly from a sense of obligation, he sprang eagerly into another phase of his career—exploration. For in exploration there was money and adventure to be had.

He was appointed to the post of commissioner to survey the long-disputed boundary between Virginia and North Carolina. In 1728 he set about the task of penetrating and mapping the westward wilderness as if the expedition were a combination of scientific field trip, military foray, religious crusade, literary junket, and house party. He insisted on bringing a chaplain along for possible baptisms along the way, and he packed enough wine to insure good spirits in spite of all hazards, natural and human.

His wilderness adventures with bears and Indians, all of which he took with unfailing good humor, were recorded in his journal—as were his observations on natural science and on the sad lot of the American frontiersmen. The edited version of this journal, called *History of the Dividing Line*, has become one of the classics of early American literature.

Before his death in 1744, Byrd also journeyed to other parts of his Virginia, and he served as one of the senior members of the council, standing second only to the council's president, the old and now deaf Commissary Blair. Though other planters may have had greater wealth and more land (Byrd ultimately owned 179,000 acres), he was indisputably the leader of his class, setting the style of what it was to be an American gentleman not only for his contemporaries but for future generations. He made it clear that to be a gentleman did not mean to cling to outmoded ideas and habits; on the contrary, many of his ideas seem astonishingly advanced. For one thing, he believed that slavery was an unhealthy force in Virginia, and he applauded the actions of Governor Oglethorpe in prohibiting rum and new slaves from being shipped into Georgia by aggressive New England merchants.

For another, he believed passionately in the westward destiny of his country, and he feared the possibility of conflict with the French in the lands beyond the crest of the Blue Ridge Mountains. He also foresaw the need to build new cities in which culture might flourish, so that the steps taken from Jamestown to Williamsburg might go on into the future. It is more than a happenstance of history that in 1737 Byrd laid out the foundations of two cities—Richmond and Petersburg. Two generations later, in the midst of a bitter war for independence, Richmond was selected as the third capital of the Commonwealth of Virginia—which would become one of thirteen stars on the flag of the future United States of America.

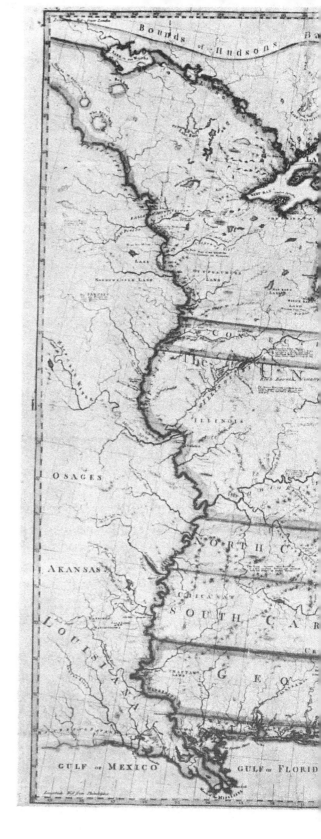

t the end of the Revolution, as this 1784 map of the new United States indi-
ates, Virginia, reaching to the Mississippi, was largest of the thirteen states.

WILLIAMS, E. *Virginia Discovery of Silk Worms,* 1650

This diagram of a Virginia saw-mill was made in 1650. The water wheel (at right) gives power to the saw (at top) by means of gears.

AMERICAN HERITAGE PUBLISHING CO., INC.

PRESIDENT JAMES PARTON

EDITOR IN CHIEF JOSEPH J. THORNDIKE, JR.

EDITORIAL DIRECTOR, BOOK DIVISION RICHARD M. KETCHUM

ART DIRECTOR IRWIN GLUSKER

AMERICAN HERITAGE JUNIOR LIBRARY

EDITOR RUSSELL BOURNE

ASSISTANT EDITOR SEAN MORRISON

ART DIRECTOR JANET CZARNETZKI

PICTURE RESEARCHER MARY LEVERTY

COPY EDITOR ELAINE ANDREWS

EDITORIAL RESEARCHER NANCY SIMON

EDITORIAL ASSISTANT BETSY SANDERS

ACKNOWLEDGMENTS

The Editors are deeply grateful to Louis B. Wright, Director of the Folger Shakespeare Library, for his guidance and advice on pictorial material and sources. They would also like to thank the following individuals and institutions for their generous advice and assistance in preparing this book:

Boston Public Library—Helen H. Sevagian
Cape Hatteras National Seashore, Manteo, North Carolina—Bruce W. Black
Colonial National Historical Park, Yorktown, Virginia—Charles E. Hatch
Colonial Williamsburg—Marguerite Gignilliat
Henry Francis Du Pont Winterthur Museum, Delaware—Dorothy Greer
Folger Shakespeare Library, Washington—Elaine Fowler
Henry E. Huntington Library and Art Gallery, San Marino—Jean Preston
Susanne Puddefoot—London
Virginia Museum of Fine Arts, Richmond
Virginia State Library, Richmond—Katherine M. Smith

FURTHER READING

Barbour, Philip L. *The Three Worlds of Captain John Smith.* Boston, Houghton, Mifflin Co., 1964.

Craven, Wesley F. *The Virginia Company of London, 1606–1624.* Williamsburg, Jamestown 350th Anniversary Historical Booklet, No. 18, 1957.

Dowdey, Clifford. *The Great Plantation.* New York, Rinehart & Company, 1957.

Fishwick, Marshall W. *Virginia, A New Look at the Old Dominion.* New York, Harper and Brothers, 1959.

Hatch, Charles E., Jr. *The First Seventeen Years: Virginia, 1607–1625.* Williamsburg, Jamestown 350th Anniversary Historical Booklet, No. 6, 1957.

Jester, Annie Lash. *Domestic Life in Virginia in the Seventeenth Century.* Williamsburg, Jamestown 350th Anniversary Historical Booklet, No. 17, 1957.

Mapp, Alf J., Jr. *The Virginia Experiment.* Richmond, The Dietz Press, 1957.

McCary, Ben C. *Indians in Seventeenth-Century Virginia.* Williamsburg, Jamestown 350th Anniversary Historical Booklet, No. 18, 1957.

Morton, Richard L. *Colonial Virginia.* 2 Vols. Chapel Hill, University of North Carolina Press, 1960.

Parks, George B. *Richard Hakluyt and the English Voyages.* New York, Frederick Ungar, 1961.

Porter, Charles W. *Fort Raleigh.* Washington, D.C., National Park Service Historical Handbook, Series No. 16, 1961.

Quinn, D. B. *Raleigh and the British Empire.* New York, Collier Books, 1962.

Rowse, A. L. *The England of Elizabeth.* New York, The Macmillan Company, 1951.

Wallace, Willard M. *Sir Walter Raleigh.* Princeton University Press, 1959.

Washburn, Wilcomb E. *Virginia Under Charles I and Cromwell, 1625–1660.* Williamsburg, Jamestown 350th Anniversary Historical Booklet, No. 7, 1957.

Wertenbaker, Thomas J. *Bacon's Rebellion, 1676.* Williamsburg, Jamestown 350th Anniversary Historical Booklet, No. 8, 1957.

Whiffen, Marcus. *The Public Buildings of Williamsburg.* Colonial Williamsburg, Inc., 1958.

Wright, Louis B. Ed. *A Voyage to Virginia in 1609.* Charlottesville, The University Press of Virginia, 1964.

———— *The First Gentlemen of Virginia.* San Marino, The Huntington Library, 1940.

INDEX

Bold face indicates pages on which illustrations or maps appear

Africa, 14
Amadas, Philip, 29, 32, 33, 35
American colonies, 13, 17, 22, 24, 29, 33, 47, 49, 86, 95, 139, 143
American Revolution, 149
"Ancient Planters," 96
Anglican Church, 11, 17, 18, 63, 140
  in colonies, 96, 104, 111, 140
Animals. See North America, Animals of
Archer, Gabriel, 60, 71, 78
Archers Hope Cove, 54
Archers Hope Creek, 117
Argall, Captain Samuel, 87, **88,** 89
Arms and armor, European, 6, **6,** 27, 36, 46, 63, 104, 106, 108, 109, **124, 125,** 128, **128–129,** 137
  Indian, **31,** 61, 63, **69, 100–101,** 108, **108, 110–111, 123**
Azores, 27
Bacon, Francis, 49, 125
Bacon, Nathaniel, 124–126, **126,** 127, 129, 132, 134, 144
Bacon's Laws, 128, 134
Bacon's Rebellion, 7, 124, 125, **125,** 126–130, 132–136, 141
Bark-Raleigh, 24
Barlow, Arthur, 29, 32
Berkeley, Governor Sir William, 120, **120,** 121, **121,** 122, 124, **124,** 125, 129, 132, 134, 136
Berkeley, Lady, 120, **120**
Bermuda Islands, 78, 81, 82, 84, 86
Binford, Julien
  painting by, **64–65**
Biscay, Bay of, 40
Blair, Commissary James, 140, 141, 147, 148
Blue Ridge Mountains, 148
Brodnax, Elizabeth, 130, **131**
Brodnax, William, 130, **131**
Burgesses, House of, 94, 95, **95,** 102, 111, 114, 120, 124, 125, 129, 132, 134, 136, 140, 144, **144**
Butts, Thomas, 11, 13
Byrd, William, 142–144, 146
Byrd, William, II, 142–148
  journals of, 147
Cabot, John, 12, 13
Cabot, Sebastian, 12, 13, **13**
Calais, France, 42
Cambridge University, 125
Canary Islands, 54, 56
Canoes, 30, 61, 62, **62,** 110, **110–111**
Cape Henry, 56, 59
Cape Horn, 21
Cape Lookout, 40
Caribbean Sea, 23, 47, 87
Carver, William, 129
Cathay (Cataia), 22
Catholicism, 17, 18, 27, 59, 118, 137
Cavaliers, 122, 125
Cavendish, Thomas, 33
Chapman, John Gadsby, 76
  painting by, **76–77**
Charles I, king of England, 115, **115,** 117, 118, 120, 122
Charles II, king of England, 125, 132, 136, 137
Charles City, Virginia, 126
Chesapeake Bay, 8, 35, 39, 40, 61, 78, 121

Chickahominy River, 66, 68, 69, 71
Coale, Griffith Baily, 52
  painting by, **52–53**
Coats of arms, 51, **51,** 68, **68,** 112, **112–113**
Colonial diseases, 40, 60, 63, 78, 83, 96, 111, 113, 126
Colonial economy, 91, 100–102, 113–115, 118, 120, 121, 124, 126, 134, 136, 139, 140, 148
Colonial education, 104, 105, **105,** 117, 140, 141, 146
Colonial government, 49–51, 59, 60, 71, 78, 81, 85, 86, 94–96, 114–121, 124–128, 132, 134, 136, 139, 140, 144, 146–148
Colonial industry, 100–102, 104, **104–105,** 107, 108, 150
Colonial society, 91, 101, 102, 139, 140–143, 145–148
Colonial taxes, 50, 96, 120, 121, 125, 128, 136, 147
Colonists, 7, 17, 35, 36, 38–42, 46, 50, 53, 54, 57–60, 65, 71, 76, **76–77,** 80, 81, 83–85, 89, 95–97, **98–99,** 99, 100, 102, 104, 105, 118, 120, 121, 136, 137, 139, 142
Colonization, 13, 21, 22, 33, 35, 39, 42, 49–51, 54, 57, 73, 74, 80, 81, 113, 114
  voyages of, 10, 24, 41, 42, 46, 47, 50, 51, 54, 57, 59, 60, 63, 74, 81, 96, 100
Commonwealth, the, 124, 127
Corn, 60, **60,** 61, 66, 71, 74, 78, 101
Couper, William, 8
  sculpture by, **title page**
Croatoan Island, 36, 38, 40, 46
Cromwell, Oliver, 122, 124
Culpeper, Governor Lord, 134, 136
Curle's Neck, Virginia, 126
Dale, Sir Thomas, **86,** 87
Dare, Eleanor, 41
Dare, Virginia, 41
De Bry, Theodore, 89
  paintings by, **62, 88, 108, 110–111**
Delaware, Lady, 90
Delaware, Thomas West, Lord, 81, 83, 85, 86, **86,** 95
Delight, 24, 25
Devon, England, 17, 21, 27
Discovery, 51, 53, 54
Doeg Indians, 126
Dover, England, 29
Drake, Francis, 17, 21, 23, 33, 36, 39
Dutch Gap, Virginia, 104, 108
East India Company, 51, 113
East Indies, 73
Edward VI, king of England, 18
Elizabeth I, queen of England, 17, 18, **18,** 22, 24, 27, 29, 30, 32, 33, 41, 46, 47, 60
  court of, 27, 29
Elizabeth City County, Virginia, 117
England, 8, 10, 12, 13, 17, 18, 21, 24, 25, 27, 29, 32, 35, 39, 41, 42, 46, 47, 48, 57, 63, 71, 74, 75, 78, 81, 87, 89, 95, 102, 103, 112, 114, 119, 120, 121, 124, 129, 134, 136, 137, 139, 143
English Channel, 42
Europe, 14, 17, 66, 68, 87, 126
Expeditions, 66, 71, 78, 147
Exploration, voyages of, 11, 13, 15, 21, 22, 24, 25, 27, 29, 33, 35, 39, 40, 51
Explorers, English, 11–13, 17, 18, 21, 24, 25, 27, 29, 30, 32, 33, 35, 38, 39, 59–61
  French, 13

Spanish, 13
Falling Creek, Virginia, 102, 104, 108
Farmers, English, 38, 39, 50, 81, **81,** 96, 121
  colonial, 126, 143
Fernandez, Simon, 29, 33, 40, 41
Florida, 13, 21, 29
Fort Raleigh, 35, **44–45,** 45, 46
Fox hunting, 146, **146**
France, 20, 27, 42, 48, 148
Frontiersmen, 125, 147
Gates, Lieutenant Governor Sir Thomas, 83, 85, 86, 87, 89
General Assembly of Virginia, 94, 95, **95,** 96, 101, 111, 114, 115, 118–120, 125, 127, 134, 137, 140, 144, 146, 147
General Court of Virginia, 144, **144,** 147
Geography, 12, 13
Georgia Colony, 148
Georgian architecture, 146
Gilbert, Sir Humphrey, 7, 21, 22, 24, 25, **25,** 27, 29
  works of, 22
Glorious Revolution, 136–138
Gloucester County, Virginia, 124, 132
Godspeed, 51, **52–53**
Gold, search for, 24, 35, 36, 39, 42, 47, 50, 51, 63, 66, 69, 71, 73, 80, 113, 121
Golden Hind, 21, 24, 25
Gosnold, Captain Bartholomew, 59, 64
Governor's Palace of Virginia, 145, **145**
Granganimeo, 30, 32, 35
Great Rebellion, 122
Green Spring plantation, 122, **122,** 124, 129
Grenville, Sir Richard, 33, **33,** 35, 36, 39, 41, 42
Hakluyt, Richard, 10–13, 17, 21, 25, 32, 39, 47, 49
  works of, 12, 13, 17
Hakluyt, Richard (cousin), 12
Hampton, Virginia, 117
Hampton Roads, Virginia, 60
Hariot, Thomas, 33, 35, 39
Harrison, Lucy, 142
  painting by, **142–143**
Harvey, Captain Sir John, 114, 117–119
Hawkins, John, 29
Henrico Corporation, 85, 89, 104, 106, 108
Henry VIII, king of England, 4, 17, 18, **19**
Hog Island, 74, 85
Holland, 22, 51, 102, 137
Hopewell, 42, 46
Howard, Governor Lord, 136, 139
Indentured servants, 91, 96, 100, 101
Indian massacres, 83, 95, 105, 106, 108, 109, **109,** 110, **110–111,** 111, 115, 122
Indians, 7, 13, 29, **29,** 30, **31,** 32–34, **34,** 35, 36, 38–41, 45, 46, 51, 56, **56,** 57, 60–62, **62,** 63–66, **67,** 68, 69, **69,** 71, **72–73,** 74, **76–77,** 78, 83, 84, 86, **88,** 89, 90, 97, **100–101,** 101, 102, 104, 105, **105,** 106, 108, **108,** 109, **109,** 110, **110–111,** 111, 117, 122, 123, **123,** 125, 126–128, 133, 144, 147
  See also Doeg Indians, Monacan Indians, Pamunkey Indians, Potomac Indians, Powhatan Confederation, Susquehannock Indians
Ireland, 22, 27, 29, 33, 42, 112

James I, king of England, 46, **46,** 47, 49, 51, 95, 113–115, 137
James II, king of England, 137
James Falls, 63, 78, 100
James Fort, **cover,** 8, 60, 63, 74, 79, **79,** 85, **85–86,** 92, **92,** 97, **110–111,** 111
James River, 7, 8, 54, **54, 55,** 56, 59, 61, 63, 65, 66, 71, 74, 78, 89, 91, 92, 97, 100–102, 108, 117, **118–119,** 119, 124, 129, 142
Jamestown, Virginia, **cover,** 7, 8, 53, 56, **56,** 60, 61, 63, 64, 66, 68, 69, 77, 78, 80, 84–86, 89, 91, 92, **92–93,** 95–97, **98–99,** 101, 104, 106, 107, 109, 111, 113–115, 126, 128–130, 132, 134, 135, 138, **138–139,** 141, 145, 148, back endsheet
Jamestown Church, 92, **93,** 94, 95, **95, 116,** 117
Jamestown colonies, 86, 89
Jamestown Island, 54, 58
Jaquelin, Edward, 130, **130**
Jaquelin, Elizabeth, 130, **130**
Jones, Elmo, 94
  paintings by, **94, 126**
Kendall, George, 59, 64
Kent, England, 54
King, Sidney, 109
  paintings by, **cover, 84, 98–99, 109,** back endsheet
King Creek, 119
Lane, Ralph, 33, 35, 36, 39, 45
Latrobe, Benjamin, 122
  painting by, **122**
Literature, American, 143
London, England, 12, 27, 50, 56, 59, 70, 73, 78, 80, 81, 83, 84, 90, 95, 96, 100, 107, 111, 113, 117, 132, 139, 140
London Company, 48–51, 63, 66, 71, 73, 80, 81, 90, 95, 100–102, 113–115
Lost Colony, the, 46, 47, 51
Magellan, Strait of, 22
Manteo, 32, 33, 41, 46
Maps, **front endsheet, 2–3,** 8, 10, **10–11,** 13, 14, **14–15,** 15, **20–21,** 21, **22–23, 30,** 33, 35, 42, **43,** 46, 48, **48–49,** 56, **57,** 61, **61,** 71, 74, **74,** 100, **100,** 147, **148–149,** 149, **back endsheet**
Martin, John, 59, 64, 71, 73, 78
Martinique, 54, 56
Mary, queen of England (Catholic), 18
Mary, queen of England (Protestant), 137, **137,** 141
Maryland Colony, 118
Matoaka. *See* Pocahontas
Mercator, 13
Merchants, British, 10, 12, 13, 17, 20, 42, 47, 49, 51, 59, 60, 95, 113, 114, 125
  Colonial, 148
Michel, Francis Louis
  paintings by, **123, 140**
Middle Plantation. *See* Williamsburg.
Mona Island, 54, 56
Monacan Indians, 106
Monica Island, 54
Moryson, Colonel Francis, 132
New England, 148
Newfoundland, 11, 24
Newport, Captain Christopher, 59, 61, 63, 64, 71, 73, 74, 76–78, 102
New World, 10, 13, 15, 21, 22, 24, 27, 29, 32, 38, 47, 49, 50, 66, 80, 81, 95, 96, 113, 114, 147
Nicholson, Lieutenant Governor

Francis, 139, 140, 147
North America, 7, 13, 14, 21, 22, 24, 25, 41, 48
  animals of, **23,** 35, 40, **40–41,** 57, 59, 79, **79**
North Carolina Colony, 29, 30, 40, 42, 45, 147
Northwest Passage, 22
Oglethorpe, Governor, 148
Old Dominion, 7
Opechancanough, 66, **67,** 68, 105, 106, 108, 109, 111, 117, 122
  massacres by, 105, 106, 108, 109, **109, 110–111,** 111, 115, 122
Orient, 15, 17, 21
Ortelius, 13
Oxford University, 11, 12, 27, 33
Pamunkey Indians, 68, 69
Panama, Isthmus of, 21
Parke, Lucy, 145, 146
Parliament, 49, 94, **95,** 95, 114, 121, 122, 136, 137
Petersburg, Virginia, 148
Philip II, king of Spain, 17, 41
Pilgrims, the, 91
Plymouth Colony, 91
Plymouth, England, 25, 42
Plymouth Sound, 10
Pocahontas, 69, 70, **70, 72–73,** 73, 87, **88,** 89, **89,** 90, 102, 104
Point Comfort, 78, 85
Portsmouth, England, 39
Portugal, 12, 13, 17, 29
Potomac Indians, 133
Potomac River, 71, 87
Pott, Dr. John, 117, 141
Powhatan, 8, 61, 63, 69, 71, 75, 89, 105
  cloak of, 75, **75**
Powhatan Confederation, 8, 68, 69, 74, **74,** 89, 105, 106, 123
Privateers, 17, 29, 32, 33, 35, 39, 41, 42, 71, 91
Privy Council, 41, 105, 139
Protestantism, 17, 27, 89, 118, 137
Puerto Rico, 54, 56
Puritans, the, 122
Pyle, Howard, 91, 121
  paintings by, **91, 121**
Raleigh, Sir Walter, 7, 13, 17, 18, 21, 24, **26,** 29, 32, 33, 35, 39, 40–42, 45, 47, **47,** 49, 87, 90
Ratcliffe, John, 54, 59, 64, 71, 74, 78, 83
Richmond, Virginia, 148
Roanoke Colony, 18, 35, 40, 41
Roanoke Island, 31, 32, 34–36, 39, 42, 45
Roanoke River, 35
Rolfe, John, 83, 86, 87, 89, 90, 91, 95, 102, 109
Rude Reply, the, 73, 80
Saint Luke's Church, Smithfield, Virginia, **116,** 117, 117
Sandys, Sir Edwin, 49, 81, **86,** 87, 90, 95, 114, 115
Santo Domingo, 23
Scotland, 112, 113, 137, 140
Sea Venture, 78, 81, 82, **82–83,** 83, 84
Shakespeare, William, 18, 83
Ships, of early exploration, 30
  English, 16, 17, 20, 21, 23, 24, 29, 30, 32, 33, 40, 42, 51, 122
  Colonial, 65, 77, 84, 85
  merchant, 10, 12
  of exploration, 12
  Spanish, 24, 27, 32, 33, 35, 42
  supply, 40, 41, 77, 78, 80, 84
  See also Privateers
Slaves, Negro, 90, 91, 103, 143, 148

Smith, Captain John, **5,** 6, **6,** 7, 8, 59, 61, 63, 64, 66, 68, **68,** 69–71, **72–73,** 73, 74, 78–81, 83, 87, 89
  coat of arms of, 27, 68, **68**
  maps by, **front endsheet,** 8, 71
South Sea, 51, 63, 66, 71, 121
Spain, 7, 12, 17, 18, 22, 33, 40, 41, 47, 48, 60, 63, 64, 87, 105, 113
Spanish Armada, 18, 41, 42
Spanish colonies, 18, 21, 39
Spencer, Lieutenant Governor Nicholas, 136
Spotswood, Lieutenant Governor Alexander, 147
Squirrel, 24, 25
Starving Time, the, 83
State House of Virginia, 141, 144, **144**
Stuart kings, 60, 119, 124, 125, 137
Susan Constant, 51, 53
Susquehannock Indians, 126
Swallow, 24
The Tempest (Shakespeare), 83
Thorpe, George, 105, 106, 108
Tidewater, the, 111, 122, 125, 129, 136
Tindall, Robert, 61
  map by, **61**
Tobacco, 47, 86, 87, 89, 90, **90,** 91, 96, 101–103, 113, 114, 118, 120, 134, 136
Tobacco planters and plantations, 86, 89, 90, **90,** 91, 102, **102–103,** 103, 106, 107, 115, 119–122, 125, 126, 134, 142, 143, 148
Topsell, Edward, 79
  paintings by, 79
Treasurer, 87
Tudor family, 17, 18
Turks, the, 68, **68**
Tyger, 33, 35
United States, 125, 148, 149
Virginia, 7, 8, 33, 40–42, 46, 49, 50, 89, 100, 103
  Virginia Colony, 50, 51, 56, 57, 61, 63, 66, 71, 78–80, 83, 87, 90, 95, 100–102, 104, 107, 112–114
  Virginia Commonwealth, 148, 149
  Virginia, Royal Colony of, 114, 119, 120–122, 124, 126, 131–134, 136, 137, 139, 140, 142, 143, 146–148, 150
Virginia Council. *See* Colonial government
Wanchese, 32, 33
Werowacomoco, 69
West, Thomas. *See* Delaware, Lord
West Indies, 21–23, 29, 33, 41, 42, 46, 51, 54, 87, 89, 91
Western Plantation, 22
Westminster, 94, **94**
Westover, 142, **142–143,** 145, 146
White, John, 33–35, 39–42, 46, 47, 79
  maps by, 35, 40, **40,** 46
  paintings by, **28, 31, 34,** 35, **36–37,** 39, 40, **40, 41**
William of Orange, king of England, 137, **137,** 139–141
William and Mary College, **134–135,** 135, 140, **140,** 141, 147
Williamsburg, Virginia, 117, 126, **126,** 128, 135, 138, 141, 144, 145, 148
Wingandacoa, 30, 33
Wingfield, Edward Maria, 59, 64, 71
Wingina, 30, 35, 36, 38
Wokoken Island (Ocracoke), 29, 33
Wren, Sir Christopher, 141
Wyatt, Governor Sir Francis, 111, 114, 115, 120
Yeardley, Sir George, 95, 102, 111
York River, 61, 69, 117, **118–119,** 119, 132